INCLUDES
**DVD**
VIDEO

# INSTALLING
# KITCHEN
# CABINETS
## MADE SIMPLE

## GREGORY PAOLINI

The Taunton Press

 The Taunton Press

The Taunton Press, Inc., 63 South Main Street, PO Box 5506, Newtown, CT 06470-5506
e-mail: tp@taunton.com

Editors: Alex Giannini and Helen Albert, Castle Hill Media, LLC
Copy editor: Diane Sinitsky
Indexer: Jim Curtis
Interior design: Susan Fazekas
Illustrator: Christopher Mills
Layout: Amy Griffin
Photographers: Gary Junken, © The Taunton Press, Inc., except: Front cover, pp. 2, 10, 24,
    34, 46, 64, 78, 88, 98: Greg Paolini; p. 5: Brian Pontolilo, courtesy of *Fine Home-
    building*, © The Taunton Press, Inc.; p. 6 (bottom): Roe A. Osborn , courtesy of
    *Fine Homebuilding*, © The Taunton Press, Inc.; p. 68 (bottom): © Olson Photo-
    graphic LLC, design by Jody Fierz; p. 71 (right): © Olson Photographic LLC
DVD Producer: Helen Albert, Castle Hill Media, LLC
DVD Editing: Gary Junken

Library of Congress Cataloging-in-Publication Data

Paolini, Gregory.
  Installing kitchen cabinets made simple / Gregory Paolini.
      p. cm. -- (Made simple)
    ISBN 978-1-60085-367-8 (pbk.)
  1.  Kitchen cabinets. 2.  Countertops. 3.  Kitchens--Remodeling--Amateurs' manuals.  I.
Title.
  TT197.5.K57P355 2011
  684.1'6--dc23
                        2011024647

Printed in the United States of America
10 9 8 7 6 5 4 3 2 1

The following manufacturers/names appearing in *Installing Kitchen Cabinets Made Simple*
are trademarks: Corian®, Formica®, Google®, KCMA®, Lee Valley® Tools, McFeeley's™,
Pozidriv®, Rockler® Woodworking and Hardware, SketchUp®, Woodcraft®, Woodworker's
Hardware®, Woodworker's Supply®

# Acknowledgments

Books and videos are anything but a solitary effort. It takes a good team to fashion all of the ideas and information into a finished project that doesn't appear cobbled together. In authoring this manuscript and video script, I've been blessed with a GREAT team, and I couldn't have done this without them. These folks deserve as much, or even more, credit than I do for the final result. My thanks to the following:

Eric Kimes, a student who became a teacher and more important, a close friend. You've helped me grow personally and professionally, when frankly, I was afraid to.

Marty and Dave Juchnowski, thanks for your never-ending faith in me and your willingness to lend a hand whenever needed. You two are family!

Butch Mack and crew for helping me get the worksite prepped for the video shoot on a moment's notice. Y'all do a great job!

The Architectural Studio and Shawn Leatherwood for generously offering advice and opportunities, and for sincerely wanting me to succeed as much as I do.

Gary Junken, who not only shoots a mean HD camera but also freely gives little bits of advice that always makes a big difference. Alex Giannini for doing his best to keep me on schedule, for keeping all the pieces in order, and for his mad skills with a water level!

Helen Albert, who was instrumental in transforming my ideas into an actual book. Helen, your vast knowledge of publishing may be exceeded only by your willingness to share and your patience in teaching me to become a better author. I can't thank you enough!

To all of the folks I've worked with at *Fine Woodworking* magazine and The Taunton Press, both past and present—you all have helped me become a better writer, photographer, and woodworker!

To my family: Mom, Frank, Jaime, David, and Jen. Your continued support and faith in me is so appreciated! I know you can't choose your family, but if I could, it would still be all of you!

And most of all, to my wife, Mona. Thank you for your patience when our projects are put on a back burner so others' projects can be completed. And especially for your insight, which still blows me away! Mona, it's true that behind every successful man is a great woman!

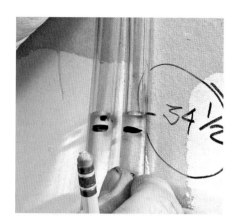

# contents

# Planning your project

**M**uch of the expense in remodeling or building a kitchen is tied up in the cabinets. One way to save some money is to install the cabinets and countertops yourself. As in every major project, a kitchen installation goes much more smoothly if you plan it carefully, beginning with choosing quality materials that fit your budget.

The cabinet on the left is a stock, off-the-shelf cabinet. It is a traditional face-frame cabinet. The one on the right is a custom-made, frameless Euro-style cabinet.

## Choosing cabinets

There are many styles of cabinets to choose from, both traditional face-frame cabinets and frameless or Euro-style cabinets. But the style is only one factor in making a choice. The materials and construction of the cabinets determine the durability and longevity of the cabinets. Quality does matter. The materials, the hardware, and finishes used can all make a significant difference in the performance of the cabinets.

### Cabinet boxes

Let's look at cabinets from opposite ends of the spectrum to help you get an idea of what to look for when buying cabinets. At one end of the spectrum is the stock economy cabinet. Economy cabinets are usually made from ½-in.-thick particleboard, covered by either paper or vinyl with wood grain printed on it. The cabinet box has plastic corner braces to add rigidity to the carcase, as well as to provide a means to attach the countertop. Staples reinforce the joints and secure them in place.

Economy cabinets often are constructed from ½-in.-thick particleboard, covered with paper or vinyl with wood grain printed on it. The plastic corner braces add rigidity to the cabinet and provide a means to attach the countertop.

The custom cabinet is made from ¾-in.-thick cabinet-grade plywood and was built to the required width of 18⅞ in. Custom cabinets can be built to any width, whereas stock cabinets come in standard sizes in increments of 3 in.

Particleboard, stapled together, provides an inexpensive solution to creating a drawer for an economy-grade cabinet. The bottom-mounted epoxy drawer slides provide easy operation for light to moderate loads.

Fully dovetailed, hardwood drawers are a sign of high quality. These sturdy drawer slides extend a full 22 in. for maximum storage and are designed to support 100 lbs.

The custom cabinet has full ¾-in.-thick hardwood veneer plywood for all of its components, including braces and countertop attachments. The interior of the cabinet is finished with a durable catalyzed lacquer, which will resist scratching and will clean up easily. The joinery is reinforced with multiple screws, ensuring it won't fail.

## Drawers

The stock economy cabinet has drawers made from particleboard, which are held together by staples. The drawer slides, or runners, are epoxy-coated steel with a set of nylon rollers, which allow the drawer to open about three quarters of its full depth.

The drawers on the custom cabinet are solid hardwood and fully dovetailed, a hallmark of quality

craftsmanship. The drawer slides are robust, designed to support 100 lbs., and they extend fully, allowing you to access the entire drawer. They slide easily and actually slide even smoother when fully loaded.

## Doors

The doors on the economy cabinet have a nice finish. They're smooth and are finished a consistent color that matches the face frame of the cabinet. They're held in place by concealed hinges, which allow for some vertical adjustment. Generally, these doors have simple cope-and-stick joinery, which has only a small area of glue surface and therefore results in a weaker frame.

The doors on the custom cabinet are constructed with true mortise-and-tenon joinery, one of the strongest methods of construction. The doors are attached to the carcase with Euro-style hinges, which are durable and offer adjustability in every direction.

## Options

A major difference between stock and semicustom cabinets versus a custom cabinet is the options available. Manufactured cabinets are usually available in widths that vary by multiples of 3 in. For example, if you need a 19-in. cabinet, you'll need to use spacers, trimmed to size, to fill any remaining space in the plan. With custom cabinets, if you need a cabinet that's $23\frac{13}{16}$ in. wide, you can get it made exactly to that measurement, which allows you to maximize the use of the space.

Another important difference is what's inside the cabinet. Most stock cabinets come with simple shelves. In the case of custom cabinets, you can get shelves, but

One of the options you'll find in better cabinets is pullouts. Unlike a shelf, you can extend a pullout to easily access the contents of the cabinet.

there are also pullouts and organizers, which make it easier and more efficient to store items in the cabinet or access heavy items stowed in the back. In stock cabinets, kits may be available for these convenience options.

## Cost

All of these differences come at a price. Custom cabinets will set you back two to three times the cost of stock cabinets, and you'll have to wait while the cabinets are being built, whereas stock cabinets are often available to drive away that day. If you add fancier doors, more options, or a more complex finish to the custom cabinet, the cost factor could reach four to five times more than the stock off-the-shelf unit.

The two options I've discussed are literally at opposite ends of the spectrum. In between are high-grade stock cabinets and semicustom cabinets built from higher-grade materials: thicker cabinet walls, solid-wood doors, better hardware, and more options. Your kitchen is a big investment, and you'll be living with it a long time. Buy the best you can afford, and remember that you're saving some money by doing the installation yourself, which could help you afford better-quality cabinets.

# Choosing countertops

Choices for countertops are even more varied. Natural stone, concrete, or solid-surface materials such as Corian® are popular and durable choices. But these materials require specialized techniques and equipment to fabricate and install them, so you should get a pro involved if you choose them for your kitchen. But there are some options that are within the reach of most do-it-yourselfers.

## Wood

In either slab or butcher-block form, wood provides a surface that is friendly to kitchen knives and can be fabricated in a home shop. But there are some draw-backs. Solid wood expands and contracts throughout the seasons, and this must be figured into the design. Wet areas adjacent to sinks are susceptible to decay, so you'll need to treat the wood or use a decay-resistant species like white oak or teak.

## Face-frame vs. frameless cabinets

In traditional, or face-frame, cabinets, the frame assembly adds strength to the cabinet box, which is typically made with thinner plywood and very often has no top at all. Euro-style cabinets are frameless. Most Euro-style cabinets employ a standardized system that allows the use of interchangeable elements, making the cabinets easier to customize. Frameless cabinets are often associated with sleek, contemporary designs, but they can be dressed up to harmonize with any style kitchen. Euro-style cabinets do have a slight advantage when it comes to spatial efficiency. Because there's no face frame to take up any space, there's more storage area. The amount saved in each box multiplied by an entire kitchen's worth of cabinetry can equate to enough "extra" space to fill a refrigerator.

Wood is an economical countertop choice that is friendly to kitchen tools. You can cut directly on the surface.

Post-form plastic laminate countertops are available at most home centers in a variety of colors and patterns. They are relatively easy to install.

Tile counters can add an old-world charm to your kitchen. The materials work easily and can be an inexpensive solution if you install it yourself.

## Tile

Tile countertops are a stylish option that you can do yourself. They provide a solid, heat-resistant surface at a reasonable price. But because of tile's hardness, knife edges will dull instantly when cut on the surface, and a dish or glass dropped from even a few inches is likely to break or even shatter. The grout around tiles is vulnerable to staining, so it must be properly sealed.

## Plastic laminate

The most common countertop choice in new kitchens is plastic laminate. Plastic laminate has been around since the 1920s. Today, there are many companies that manufacture it, but it's still popularly known as Formica®, which is the brand name of the originator of the product.

You can buy straight runs of stock plastic laminate countertops with an integrated backsplash and drip edge. Known as post-form countertops, these just need to be cut to length and finished at the end with a matching kit. Post-form countertops are inexpensive and readily available from most home centers and kitchen cabinet shops. You can also have a custom plastic laminate counter fabricated, or even build one yourself with a modest array of tools and skills (see pp. 84–87).

## Other considerations

Regardless of the type of countertop you choose, you'll need to consider the weight of the material. Concrete countertops are extremely heavy, while plastic laminate countertops are relatively light. Check with the countertop supplier to find out how much the countertops will weigh before making your cabinet purchase and be sure to buy sufficiently sturdy cabinets.

Price is another thing to consider, especially if you're trying to adhere to a set budget. Consulting with a countertop specialist or fabricator can help to answer questions regarding price, durability, stain and heat resistance, and more. If you end up in the situation where your budget will only allow for either high-quality cabinets or your dream counters, my advice is to go with the high-quality cabinets and choose a less expensive counter. Later on, you can upgrade the countertops. However, replacing the cabinets and attempting to reuse the existing countertops is almost impossible.

Collaborating with professionals, such as architects and interior designers, can help you develop a beautiful and efficient kitchen. Their specialized training and experience can save you from making expensive mistakes.

## Designing the kitchen

Your kitchen is one of the key factors in determining your home's value. And when you add up the cost of cabinets, appliances, and other materials, it's probably one of the most expensive rooms in your home. So it makes sense to develop a good design, not only to maximize your investment but also to make life in the kitchen easier and more enjoyable.

If I were to dedicate every page of this book to design, I would only scratch the surface. Fortunately, there are many resources available to you including countless magazine articles and books on the subject. Some of these resources are listed on p. 106.

If your budget allows, get a professional involved in the design process. Architects and interior designers have specialized training and in-depth education that can be invaluable for successfully designing a functional and attractive kitchen. Another option is to collaborate with an experienced cabinetmaker to help ensure that your final design is a winner. If you choose to get your cabinets from a home center or a builder's-supply house, most have design software available, coupled with experienced kitchen designers to help you make smart choices.

You can use computer software to design your dream kitchen. Some drawing programs can be downloaded from the Internet for free. Here, I'm using SketchUp®, a free drawing program from Google®.

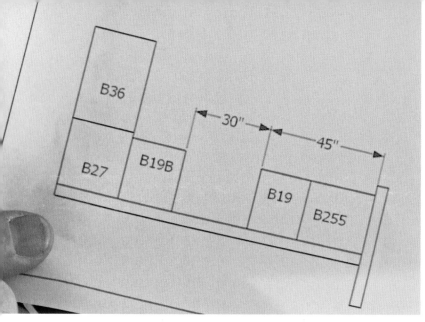

A carefully annotated plan in which each cabinet has a unique code is essential to a smooth cabinet installation.

programs that allow you to build your virtual kitchen, so you can experiment with layout and even change the colors and wood species of your cabinets. You can render a true three-dimensional view of your kitchen, completely to scale, and take a tour before you even touch a real cabinet.

The important point here is that you must have a detailed plan carefully worked out before you buy or build cabinets or install them. Make sure you measure out the space accurately and keep track of your measurements. Also, remember that the walls and floor may not be flat or plumb, so take that into account when determining cabinet sizes. You may also need to figure in filler material for corners where the wall is not plumb.

As you draw your plan, figure in the exact cabinet sizes. Give each cabinet in your plan a unique code so that when the time comes to match cabinets with the plan, there's no ambiguity. I use "B" for base cabinets and "W" for wall cabinets followed by the cabinet widths. If there is more than one cabinet of the same width, I assign them successive letters: A, B, C, etc.

You can design your kitchen yourself as well. The catalogs available from home centers and cabinet shops are great resources. They can provide design and layout ideas. Some cabinet manufacturers provide free software or online tools to help you lay out the kitchen using stock cabinet sizes. There are also low-cost, even free, drawing

## Plan for the kitchen

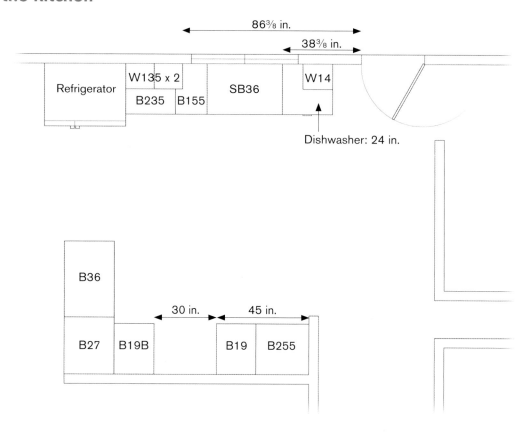

It doesn't hurt to select appliances while you're choosing the cabinets and drawing up your plan. That way, you'll be sure that everything will fit after the cabinets are installed.

Don't forget to choose decorative hardware. Your choices are nearly limitless. I use pulls from the same family and finish but in graduated sizes to create more visual interest.

### Design considerations

As you develop a design for your kitchen, here are a few things to keep in mind. First, consider how you work in the kitchen and the areas you travel to and from regularly while preparing a meal. The plan on the facing page is for our project kitchen. In developing the plan, I tried to keep the sink, refrigerator, and stove in close relation to one another so travel between these points will be minimized, making food preparation and cleanup easier.

Or you may opt for "work zones," where actions or functions are grouped into specific areas within the kitchen. You may have a food-prep zone, a storage zone, and a cleanup zone. And don't forget an area for a small kitchen office or a couple of small cabinets to store cookbooks. Plan for a place to set a laptop so you can track down your favorite online recipes.

One of the best pieces of advice I can offer is to develop a budget for your kitchen. Cabinets and countertops are just one aspect of the project. Relocating plumbing, sinks, walls, and electricity can have a big impact on the financial scope of the project, so figure in everything.

## Appliances and accessories

Generally, appliances are designed to fit into standard openings, with the actual appliance slightly undersized so they'll slip right in. Stoves are commonly 30 in. wide, while dishwashers generally have a width of 24 in. and a height that accommodates a standard countertop. Refrigerator sizes, on the other hand, vary widely, so you

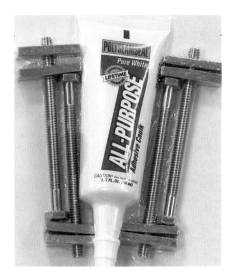

Make sure to order any kits you'll need for your installation. If you're joining mitered post-form countertops, make sure to get the installation kit. Also, remember to get any end-of-run or buildup kits you may need.

may want to have a specific one in mind, or design the space so that it will fit most models. To be safe, check the manufacturer's website, and download its product manuals and installation guides for exact dimensions and specifications. If the cabinets will require modification for appliances such as a hood-microwave combination, it's helpful to know beforehand.

Also, consider the decorative hardware you'll need to open and close the cabinet drawers and doors and whether you'll need extended screws for installation. For countertop installation, you may need some kits for end-of-run applications, to build up to standard height, or to join mitered corners. Have these on hand before you begin installing the countertops to avoid trips to the store or having to order them and waiting until they come in.

# Preparing the site

**W**hether you're working in a new home during construction or have just removed all the old cabinets and appliances as part of a renovation, one of the first things you'll need to do is establish reference points for installing the cabinets. You'll want to transfer every measurement on your plan to the site. This step will ensure that the cabinets will fit exactly as intended with no surprises.

In this chapter, you'll learn about the basic layout lines you'll need to indicate on the walls and floor of the site to locate the cabinets. You'll learn how to find reference points so the cabinets all around the kitchen will be on the same plane. I'll also show you how to mark the walls and floors so that locating the cabinets during installation is quick and easy. And I'll show you a foolproof method for laying out a square for locating freestanding cabinetry.

## Horizontal reference lines

All of the horizontal layout lines (for example, the position of the wall cabinets) and the top of the base cabinets are measured from the floor. In the virtual kitchen represented in your plan, all of the corners are

Finding the highest point of the floor in the room is the first step in laying out your cabinetry. From this point, you'll reference all of your installation heights.

square, the walls are plumb, and the floors are level. Rarely, if ever, are real kitchens level or plumb, even in brand-new homes. Assuming that the floor is not perfectly level, you'll want to start your layout by finding the highest point of the floor.

I like to work from the highest point in the room for two reasons. First, it's more efficient just to shim a cabinet up to a line, rather than to cut or scribe a cabinet so it fits down to a layout line, which is what you would need to do if you based your layout off of the low point in the floor. Second, some built-in appliances need a minimum height to be installed. If necessary, the appliance can be shimmed up, but it's nearly impossible to cut or scribe an appliance down to fit if it's too tight.

### Finding the highest point

You can find the highest point of the floor in a number of ways. You can use a long spirit level and "step it out" around the perimeter of the room. Or you can establish a level line around the room with a laser level or water level and measure down to the floor. In this method, the smallest measurement will indicate the highest point of the floor.

Once all of the installation heights have been established around the room, connect the points with a chalkline for quick reference.

A water level is a simple and effective way to establish a level line and excels at establishing level points across a room. A laser level is a high-tech tool to accomplish the same task. A laser beam shoots a level mark around the room. Measuring down from the laser line will allow you to find the highest point of the floor.

## Marking off the horizontal reference lines

Once you've established the highest point of the floor, begin laying out your horizontal reference lines. In most kitchens, countertop height is 36 in. Countertops are planned to be 1½ in. thick. Subtracting the countertop thickness from the overall height leaves 34½ in. This is the height to the top edge of the base cabinets. Mark it on the wall at the location of the highest point.

The next most important height is where the upper cabinets begin. Generally, upper cabinets are located 18 in. above the countertop. This clearance will accommodate most small appliances and leave room for food preparation and other kitchen tasks. Adding 18 in. of open space to the countertop height puts the bottom edge of the upper cabinets at 54 in. If you have appliance cabinets or other accessories, include the heights of these elements in your layout.

You'll need to transfer the horizontal measurements around the room, wherever you'll be installing cabinets. This can be done with a laser level, but it requires precise setup to properly align the laser beam with your elevation marks. If you have an extra pair of hands, it's actually quicker to use a water level. You can also use a long spirit level to establish the two points. Continue around the room as dictated by your plan. Then snap a chalkline between points to mark off each of your horizontal layout lines.

Base cabinets are generally 34½ in. high to accommodate a 1½-in.-thick countertop. Transfer the 34½-in. measurement to the wall as a horizontal reference line.

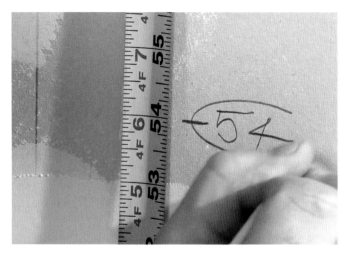

Upper cabinets begin at 54 in. off the floor, providing 18 in. of space between the upper cabinets and the countertop.

If you have an extra pair of hands, you can use a water level to find the highest spot and then use it to lay out your horizontal lines. A water level is simply a piece of plastic tubing filled with water and two marks drawn with magic marker to indicate the point where the water finds its level.

## Vertical reference lines

The next step in the layout process is to add the vertical lines. These lines indicate where the edges of the cabinets will be located and where adjacent cabinets will come together. The vertical lines will help you when positioning and installing the cabinets, but more important, they ensure that all the cabinets will fit exactly where they should be.

Depending on your design, you'll either have cabinets with an open end of run or cabinets that abut a wall. Each situation needs to be approached a little differently. On an open end of run the cabinets will just "begin" at some point. You'll need to make sure you define where that point is or a point relative to it. Refer back to your plan and identify the hard reference points, for example, the location of an entry door or the center of a window under which you'll position the sink. Assuming you have a 36-in. sink base, and your plan calls for the sink to be centered under the window, your cabinet will extend 18 in. on each side of the center mark.

Make your marks on the corresponding horizontal line you drew earlier. Use a spirit level to extend these lines as far as you'll need them for installation. For a base cabinet, that means from the floor to the 34½-in. horizontal line. For a wall cabinet, extend the line from the 54-in. mark up to the top of the cabinet, usually 30 in. to 36 in. Don't extend vertical lines beyond the horizontal layout

### Figuring in floor height

If your kitchen has an existing finished floor, you don't need to make any adjustments. If you're installing sheet vinyl or vinyl tile squares, which are very thin, you can ignore the difference. But if you're working from a subfloor and plan to install hardwood flooring, ceramic tile, or stone laid on backer board, you'll need to raise your horizontal layout lines by an amount equal to the thickness of your finished floor. Your flooring contractor or supplier can give you more details on what the height adjustment should be.

Determining the slope of adjacent walls is critical in laying out your cabinetry. Failure to do so could result in cabinets that don't fit the space designated for them.

After the measurements for vertical layout points have been transferred to the wall, draw plumb lines using a long spirit level.

Reveals between the edges of face frames and the side of a cabinet can be significant. Draw additional vertical layout lines to represent the reveal. This allows the cabinet box to line up with layout lines and ensures more accurate placement.

lines. On painted walls, drawing extra lines just means more cleanup later.

With the first cabinet laid out, refer to your plan and transfer adjacent cabinet widths to the wall until you've laid out the run. Mark the location with the cabinet number and letter in the plan. Once the positions of all the cabinets have been transferred, make sure the sink cabinet is lined up over the plumbing and the dishwasher and other appliances are where they're supposed to be. This final check will eliminate surprises when you start hanging the cabinets.

For cabinets that butt against a wall in a corner, you already have a fixed, immovable point where you'll begin your layout. But before you start transferring vertical lines, you'll need to verify the plumb of the wall to see whether it leans toward the cabinets or away from them. If the wall leans away from the cabinets, it means the bottom of the wall will contact the cabinet, and you'll have a gap at the top. If the wall leans toward them, you'll have contact at the top of the cabinet and a gap at the bottom. It's really important to start your measurements from the contact point between the wall and the cabinet. If you don't, your cabinets may not fit properly. You can install a trim strip later to cover any gaps.

Once you know where your wall contact point is, measure off your cabinets and appliances, marking their location on the wall. Draw the verticals along the way.

It's important to remember that the vertical lines you've drawn represent the overall width of the cabinets. If you're installing traditional cabinets with face frames, you'll want to indicate the reveal between the face frame and the cabinet box with additional vertical lines so that the back of the cabinet box can be positioned against a layout line during installation.

## workSmart

Use multiple color chalklines to indicate the different layout lines. For example, use red for horizontal lines and blue for studs. That way, it's less likely you'll confuse stud lines with cabinet placement lines, which are usually drawn in pencil. If you're installing face-frame cabinets, use a third color to distinguish cabinet box lines from face-frame lines.

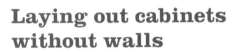

Peninsula cabinets or islands should be laid out on the floor. Use a level as a straightedge and be sure your lines remain square to adjacent walls.

## Laying out cabinets without walls

In many kitchens, there are freestanding cabinets or cabinets that jut out from a wall but are not necessarily secured to one. We usually refer to these as peninsulas or dog legs, if they come out from the wall at an angle.

Even though the back of the cabinet won't be against a wall, you need to lay out where the cabinets will be placed. And you want to make sure that they're square to the primary run of cabinets or the wall. There's no wall to draw on, so just draw lines on the floor to indicate the cabinet's location. You can then draw offset lines to indicate the toe kick, or cabinet support. To ensure that the layout lines are square to the wall, use an extra-large builder's square or use a 3-4-5 triangle (see p. 22).

## Locating studs

At this point, all of the cabinet locations should be indicated on the walls or floor. The last step of layout is to identify and mark the locations of the studs to which you'll attach the cabinets. If you're lucky, you'll have drywall that hasn't been primed, and you can see all the nail and screw holes where the wallboard is fastened to the studs. If that's the case, just snap a chalkline from the floor to the ceiling, following the line of drywall screws. Mark every stud that rests behind a cabinet.

If your walls are painted, you'll have to locate the studs. You can use electronic or magnetic stud finders. Or find them by tapping on the wall and listening for variations in tone. Once you find a stud, verify the location by driving a screw through the drywall into the stud. A screw that just spins has not found a home. If the driving resistance increases as the screw is driven farther, you've most likely driven into a wall stud.

Once you've found a single stud, you can measure off for the rest of them. Standard stud spacing is 16 in. on center. Newer homes, framed with 2x6 exterior walls, may have 24-in. on-center spacing. And while it's not too common, you may encounter interior walls with studs spaced every $19\frac{3}{16}$ in. That's the reason for the little diamonds you'll find on some tape measures.

Verify every stud that will hold cabinet screws by driving a screw into it. If you meet resistance, it's probably a stud.

# Finding the highest point with a level

I prefer to reference everything from the high point in the floor because you can easily shim cabinets or appliances up to the correct height.

1. **Step out the floor** using a long spirit level. A level 6 ft. or longer will bridge the low points in the floor and rest only on the high points. Check the floor at the wall and about 20 in. away, toward the center of the room.

2. **Keep a tally of high areas,** making notations on the wall as you go. Return to the highest point and mark it. Measure up from the floor to a height of 34½ in. (top of the base cabinets) and at 54 in. (bottom of the wall cabinets).

3. **Extend the horizontal reference lines** from your marks at the high point using a level. Or find level points working out from the starting point and snap a chalkline between them.

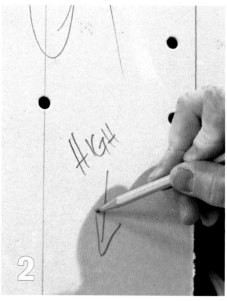

# Finding the highest point from a level reference

A water level and a laser level are very different in terms of technological sophistication, but finding the highest point of the floor works the same for both. Basically, you're establishing a level line around a room, then measuring down to find the high areas. The shortest distance between the line and the floor is the highest point. Use this method if your cabinetry will be placed on nonadjacent walls.

1. **Establish a level reference line** around the room using a laser level or water level (see p. 18.) The height of this line is not critical.

2. **Measure down from the level line** and record the measurements. Look for the shortest distance to the floor. This will be the highest point. Mark off your horizontal reference lines from this point.

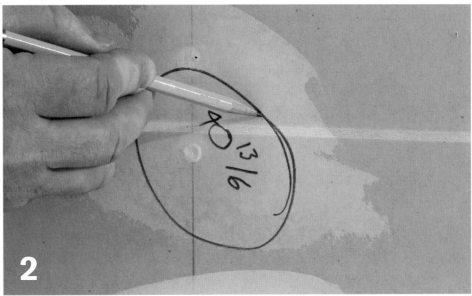

# Using a water level

A water level is just a long piece of clear tubing (available at hardware stores) filled with water. Water will naturally seek its own level. To see more easily where the level falls, you can add a drop of food coloring to the water.

1. **Allow the water to level itself.** Draw a line on the plastic tubing with permanent marker.

2. **Hold one end of the level on a reference mark.** Place the other end in the corner of the room and raise and lower it until the water lines up with the marks on both tubes and the mark on the initial wall. Mark off this location.

3. **Repeat the procedure** for each wall in the room.

4. **Mark off the horizontal reference points** in the same way around the room. Snap a line between reference points. (The photo shows the horizontal reference line for the bottom of the wall cabinets at 54 in.)

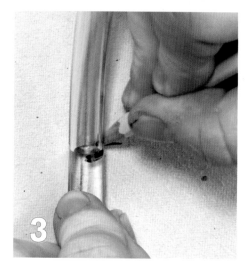

# Laying out horizontal reference lines

The horizontal layout lines indicate heights at which base cabinets and wall cabinets are installed. For base cabinets, this height is 34½ in. This allows 1½ in. for the typical countertop, bringing the top of the installed base cabinets to the standard height of 36 in. Wall cabinets are usually placed 18 in. above the countertop, or 54 in. from the floor. This leaves plenty of room for countertop appliances, yet still keeps upper cabinets within easy reach for access.

1. **Establish the high point in the floor** by using the method you prefer.

2. **Indicate the installation heights.** From the high point, mark installation heights at 34½ in. and 54 in. If you have cabinets that will be installed at heights other than those two standards, add those measurements to your layout as well.

3. **Wrap the key elevation points around the perimeter of the room.** The easiest way to do this is with a water level, although a long spirit level works as well. Lasers are more finicky in this situation because they have to be adjusted to the exact height needed. "Draw" the horizontal lines by connecting the layout marks with a chalkline.

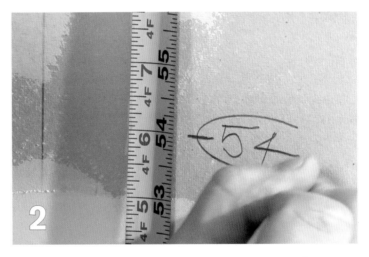

# Laying out vertical reference lines

The vertical layout lines represent the overall width of each cabinet or appliance in your design. The vertical references give you a full-scale layout of where your cabinets will be placed, ensuring that there are no surprises during the actual installation process.

1. **Establish a hard reference point.** Items such as entry doors, walls, and windows are hard points that cannot be moved. These serve as good starting points to lay out a cabinet run, especially where cabinets don't abut a wall. A sink base centered under a window is a good example. The extents of the cabinet represent the starting points for the adjacent cabinets.

2. **Determine the slope of adjacent walls.** You'll need to determine if a wall slopes toward or away from a cabinet to find the starting point for a run that butts against a wall. Begin your vertical lines at the contact point.

3. **Transfer the cabinet widths from your plan to the walls.** Use a spirit level to draw plumb lines.

4. **Indicate the code from the plan for the cabinet.** Also indicate the position of fixed appliances such as stoves, refrigerators, and built-in microwaves.

5. **Mark off the position of islands or peninsulas** on the floor. Use the 3-4-5 triangle method described on p. 22 to ensure that the layout remains square.

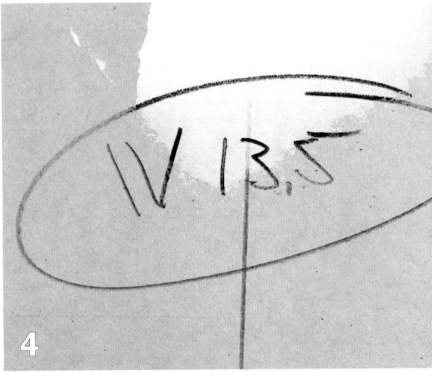

Remember the reveal. On traditional face-frame cabinets, the reveal between the face frame and the cabinet side needs to be taken into account. Draw both vertical reference lines so you can accurately position the cabinet box during installation.

# Laying out a 3-4-5 triangle

**T**he 3-4-5 isn't a tool you're likely to find at a home center or even a specialty supplier, but the good news is you already have one. The 3-4-5 refers to the ratio of the lengths of the sides of a right triangle. The ratio is the critical part, not the length. So a 3-4-5-in. triangle would work, as well as a 3-4-5-meter triangle. Multiples held to the same ratio will also work. So if you don't have enough room for 3 ft., and 3 in. is too small, multiply by a number. Using 5, for example, will give you a 15-20-25-in. triangle. As long as you stay true to the 3-4-5 ratio, everything will work out square, and you can find perpendicular layout lines for anything you wish to build, from tiny to enormous.

1. **Identify the starting point,** such as where the corner of a peninsula will begin on a wall. Lay a yardstick against the wall, anchored at that point. Then anchor a chalkline to the same point, and extend it 4 ft. If you have a 4-ft. ruler, that works even better than a chalkline.

2. **Complete the triangle with a tape measure,** placing one end of the tape at the end of the 3-ft.-long yardstick mark and lining up the 5 ft. on the tape with the 4-ft. mark of the chalkline or ruler.

3. **Line up all three points so they intersect exactly,** and you have a 3-4-5 triangle with a perfectly square corner. Then just snap the chalkline to lay out a perpendicular line.

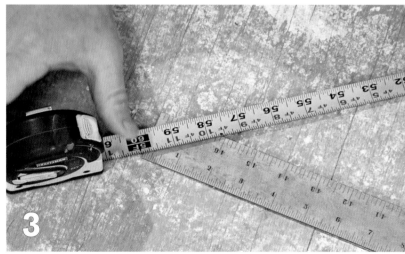

# Marking studs

Ŷou can try locating studs using the old-school method of tapping or knocking on the wall. Tapping directly over a stud produces a sharper, higher-pitched sound. Or use a stud finder. Stud finders vary from simple magnets that move on a pivot to miniature sonar devices that can practically see inside the wall. They also vary in quality and operation. Buy the best you can afford. Most electronic stud finders beep or light up when you pass the detector over a stud. Better models will indicate the perimeter of the stud and its center as well.

1. **Locate the studs** using a stud finder or by tapping the walls. Determine the center of the stud and mark it.

2. **Verify the stud location** by driving a screw into the wall at that point. A screw driven through drywall and into a void will spin with no resistance. A screw that hits a stud will turn harder after it passes through the drywall.

3. **Mark the stud location with a chalkline.** Choose a color that distinguishes stud lines from cabinet lines. In this case, I used a blue chalkline.

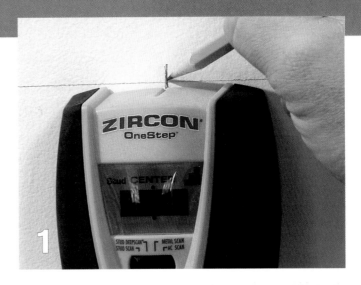

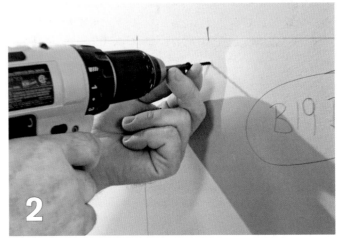

# 3

# Preparing cabinets

O nce the layout is complete, you're nearly ready to start installing the cabinets. But cabinets are heavy, and the bigger they are and the higher the quality, the more they weigh. Add accessories like pullouts and they're heavier still. So to make installation easier on your back, it's smart to prep them by stripping them down to their bare basics—an empty box.

In this chapter, I'll show you different types of cabinet hardware and the methods for removing the components they operate. You'll learn how to detach doors and drawers. Plus, I'll show you simple ways to keep all those parts organized. When it comes time to hang the cabinets, matching the cabinet with its location will be easy, and you'll be able to join up the right drawers, doors, and other parts with their respective cabinets.

## Staying organized

Stock and semicustom cabinets usually ship from the manufacturer in large cardboard boxes. Begin by removing one cabinet at a time and verifying the dimensions of the cabinet, most importantly the width, to be certain it matches your plan. You'll also want to make sure any

Carefully remove the cabinets from their packing material. Be sure the cabinets are undamaged, and contain all of the components specified on the package, including any hardware, shelves, or other accessories.

options such as pullouts or accessories are included as well, although keep in mind that some accessories may be in separate cardboard boxes. Once you've verified the size of the cabinet and made sure it has all of its parts, mark it off on your plan.

Before removing any components, label all of the parts for individual cabinets so reassembly later will be easier. Apply painter's tape to inconspicuous areas of the cabinet, doors, drawers, pullouts, shelves, and any other component that can be removed. Then mark each with a designation that matches the plan. For example, a 15-in.-wide wall cabinet will be labeled "W15." Each designation should be unique to that particular cabinet and all of its components; this way, none of the parts will get mixed up with another cabinet. So if your plan has two W15 wall cabinets, you'll want to assign an A or B suffix. And for cabinets with multiple doors, I add an L

Once you've verified that the cabinet is the correct width and height, check it off the drawing, and move on to the next.

Use a coding system that matches the cabinet codes on your plan. I use codes indicating whether the cabinet is a base or wall cabinet and its width in inches. For multiples of the same width, use letter suffixes to distinguish them. Mark all parts of the cabinets including doors, drawers, accessories, and hardware.

or an R suffix beyond that. Multiple doors beyond a pair or drawer cabinets can be indicated with numbers. With drawers, start from the top and work down.

With all the parts labeled, you can begin removing components and setting them aside. Some components, such as shelves, are a no-brainer. They just slip out. Drawers may require some finessing. Don't just yank them out.

The most efficient way to store the drawer boxes is to move them out of the way and stick them on a couple of 2x4s. Stack the drawers angled at 90 degrees to one another. This will help to avoid damaging or marring the bottom of the overhanging false front attached to the drawer.

Once all of the components have been removed, the cabinets are significantly lighter and easier to move. Additionally, these steps help protect the cabinets by placing the show parts, such as doors, drawer fronts, and finish panels, out of harm's way during the installation, when things could get bumped around and damaged.

## workSmart

Painter's tape is great for labeling components. The green color of this brand offers great visibility, and the tape releases without leaving behind residue.

The best way to keep track of small parts such as shelf pins and screws is to seal them in a plastic bag and keep them in the cabinet to which they belong.

To keep small parts together, you could just throw them in a box. But I place the loose fasteners, shock absorbers, shelf pins, and any other small parts into a sandwich-size bag and tape it to the corresponding door with painter's tape. That way, the small parts won't get lost. When the time comes to reassemble that particular cabinet, everything is conveniently right there, all together in the bag.

## Removing doors

The simplest type of door to remove is the kind outfitted with a cup or Euro-style clip hinge. You just pull a little lever at the back, and the hinge body separates from its mounting plate. These doors literally disconnect from the cabinet box in seconds.

But not every cup hinge is the clip type. You may need to loosen a screw to separate the hinge body from the plate. The screw you're looking for is usually the one that is farthest back on the hinge. Back it off a few turns, and the hinge should loosen and separate.

Many traditional-style cabinets use a version of the cup hinge that mounts directly to the face frame. In this case, the center fastener (usually a screw) is most often the part to remove.

It's important to note that if your cabinet has soft-closing hinges, there may be a small shock absorber mounted to the body of the hinge. These usually just pop right off, allowing access to the fasteners under them.

Clip-type cup or Euro-style hinges release instantly upon pulling a lever at the back of the hinge arm.

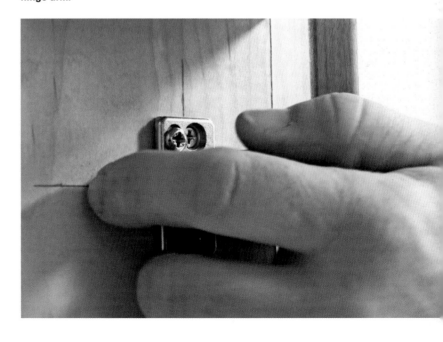

**Before the introduction of the clip-type hinge, Euro-style hinges mounted to a base plate with a single fastener at the back of the arm.**

Other than cup hinges, the other most common hinge is a standard barrel-style hinge. These are almost always used on traditional cabinetry and are simply screwed to the cabinet door and face frame with Phillips-head screws. To remove doors with barrel hinges, just unscrew the hinge fasteners. Be sure to support the weight of the door while removing the fasteners to avoid damaging any part of the cabinet or bending the hinge with the weight of the door.

**Cup hinges used on traditional cabinetry are held in place by a single screw driven into the face frame. Remove the screw, and the hinge comes free.**

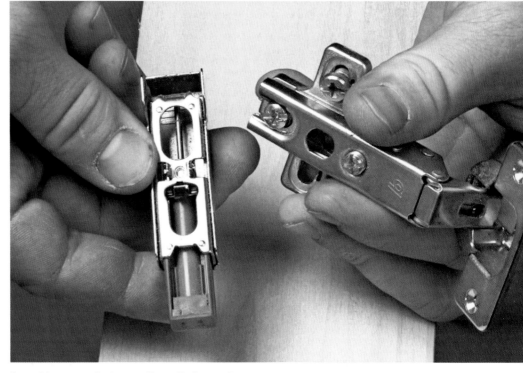

**Some hinge manufacturers offer soft-close units, which clip on to the top of the hinge arm. Pop the little shock absorber off to access the fasteners below it.**

## Pozidriv® vs. Phillips screwdrivers

**E**uro-style hinge manufacturers have embraced a fastener designed to resist stripping and cam-out (when the screwdriver slips out of the screw). This design also helps to ensure longer service life for the hardware. This special fastener almost looks like a standard Phillips-head screw, but it's actually a Pozidriv fastener. The telltale sign that marks the difference between Pozidriv and Phillips-drive screws is a little embossed X, offset from the driver recess.

Standard #2 Phillips screwdrivers may fit, but they can round out the driving flats of the fastener. Pozidriv screwdrivers provide a more positive fit, allowing you to exert more force while driving the fastener without stripping out the head. Rather than risk stripping out the screws, make sure to use the right driver for your hardware. Pozidriv screwdrivers are available directly from hinge manufacturers, as well as from cabinet-supply houses and specialty woodworking suppliers. You may also find them in some well-stocked hardware stores and some auto-parts stores.

**The secondary X embossed in the head of this fastener designates it as a Pozidriv screw.**

**The driver on the left is a standard Phillips, and the one on the right is a Pozidriv. Notice the contoured edges of the Pozidriv head, which engages the fastener better.**

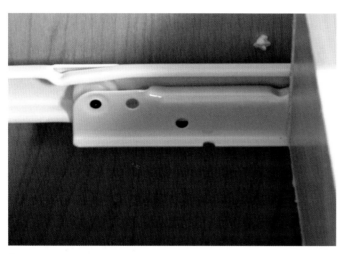

Epoxy-coated Euro-style slides generally open three-quarters of the cabinet's depth before encountering a detent. Continuing to pull the drawer, while lifting it slightly, allows removal.

Fully extending a side-mount slide will expose its release button or lever. Once it is depressed, the drawer can be removed.

# Removing drawers

There are three styles of commercial slides that are commonly used on drawers and pullouts today: Euro-style slides, side-mount slides, and fully concealed undermount slides. Let's take a look at how to remove drawers outfitted with these popular slides.

## Euro-style slides

The simplest are epoxy-coated slides, often called Euro-style slides, which mount where the bottom and side of the drawer come together. Just pull the drawer out and when it stops, lift the front edge of the drawer slightly while you continue pulling the drawer forward to get past the detent. The drawer will then come free of its mating component and pull right out of the cabinet.

## Side-mount slides

There are many variations of this style of drawer slide. Some have self-closing or soft-closing features. Other types are "over travel" in design, which allows the drawer to open to, or even beyond, the edge of the countertop.

Side-mount slides usually have a button or lever that is exposed when the drawer is fully opened. Removing

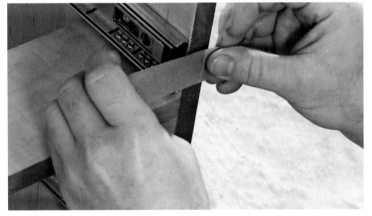

Drawer slides have a tendency to roll out once the drawer is removed. Wrapping them with painter's tape prevents them from inadvertently moving during installation.

the drawer is as simple as depressing this button. This separates the slide, allowing the drawer to pull free.

Once the drawer is out, push the slides back in, and wrap some painter's tape around the end of the slide. This will keep it from inadvertently extending during cabinet installation.

## Undermount slides

The third type of slide in common use today is the undermount slide. These are a premium slide. Not long ago, you would only find them in high-end cabinetry. Today, they're popular because they are hidden from view in use and usually incorporate self-closing and soft-closing features. They've become so popular that they can be found even on many entry-level cabinets.

To separate the drawer from an undermount slide, simply open the drawer, reach under the front of it, and squeeze the handles on the bottom of the drawer to release it. The drawer box will lift out and disengage from the slides. Then just push the cabinet-mounted slide back in, and if equipped with a self-closing mechanism, the slide will retain this position during installation.

Once the large orange handle of this undermount-style runner is depressed, the drawer box will come free from the slide.

# Prepping cabinets for installation

Removing components from cabinets makes them lighter and easier to maneuver during the installation process. It also helps to protect you because there won't be any doors to swing open and strike you unexpectedly. Drawers that remain installed in base cabinets could extend while tilting, causing a cabinet to become off-balance, tip over, and get damaged as well as injure you.

1. **Remove the cabinets from their packaging.** As you unwrap them, verify that they are correct according to your plan. Make sure all components are included as well. Remove shelves and supports. Place small components such as shelf pins in a small plastic bag, taped to the cabinet door.

2. **Measure the cabinet width** to confirm it, and check off that cabinet on your plan.

3. **Label all parts.** Use painter's tape and a marker, writing the cabinet number on all components. For example, use "B24" to indicate a 24-in.-wide base cabinet or "W30" for a 30-in.-wide wall cabinet.

4. **Remove the doors.** Stack them aside, out of the way for the remainder of the cabinet installation process.

5. **Remove the drawers and pullouts.**

6. **Store drawers on 2x4s,** stacking each drawer on the other at 90 degrees so the bottom edges of the faces won't be damaged and the drawers won't topple.

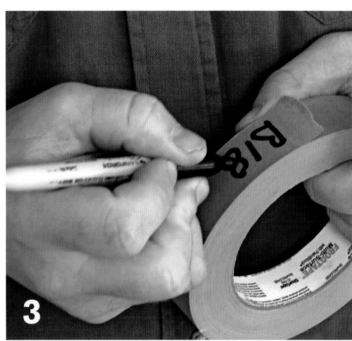

# Installing wall cabinets

Because all of the walls are still bare, it may seem as though you're still at the beginning of the process. But all of the steps you've taken so far will help to make your job easier, quicker, and more efficient.

Some cabinet installers like to tackle the base units first. I prefer to start with the wall cabinets. That way, I don't have to reach over big, bulky base cabinets while anchoring the wall cabinets. I also don't have to distort my body or twist my back. And there are no base cabinets to get in the way of the stepladders I'll need to get to the top of the wall cabinets.

In this chapter, I'll show you several methods for attaching cabinets to walls securely. You'll learn a simple way to support the weight of the cabinets during installation. If you're working alone, this support system will allow you to position and fasten the cabinets accurately. And you'll also learn techniques to ensure a straight, flat run of cabinets, one of the marks of a professional installation.

The nailing strip is an integral part of most cabinets. It provides a place to locate fasteners, as well as the structural strength to hold the cabinet and contents on the wall.

## Attaching the cabinets

Most cabinets have simple nailing strips, integrated into the cabinet assembly. These serve as the backbone to attach the cabinet to the wall. Fasteners are driven through these nailers, the drywall, and finally anchor into the studs in the wall, holding the cabinet, and all of its contents, in place.

### Cabinet screws

It's important to use screws that are not only strong enough to support the cabinet but also long enough to do the job. Long drywall screws won't cut it here; they just don't have the tensile strength for the task and can break under load. Instead, use 3-in.-long cabinet-installation screws.

It's equally important that the screws anchor into studs. A fastener run into drywall has no holding

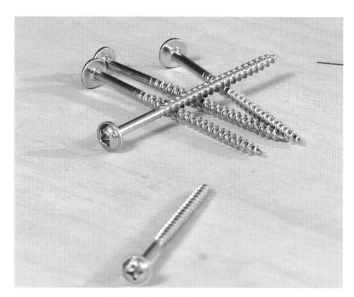

Cabinet-installation screws have strong steel shanks and deep threads that bite into the wall studs, providing ample support.

**workSmart**

In a pinch, you can use superstrong 3-in.-long exterior steel decking screws combined with finish washers.

These European-style cabinets are ganged together with 1¼-in. screws driven through their sides. Clamps ensure things don't move during the process.

strength. Because some cabinets can be narrower than the standard stud spacing, you could end up with no stud positioned behind your cabinet. In this case, you'll want to make sure there's blocking installed to fasten the cabinet (see the sidebar on the facing page). Securing cabinets with screws passing through integrated nailing strips into studs is the most common way to hang upper cabinets, but there are other methods.

### French cleats

Usually shopmade from ¾-in.-thick hardwood or plywood, French cleats are simply a pair of interlocking pieces of wood whose edges are cut to 45 degrees. One cleat is mounted to the back of a cabinet and the other to the wall. When the cabinet is placed on the cleat, the weight of the cabinet pulls the angles into close contact, providing a secure connection to the wall. French cleats are great for applications where cabinets may need to be moved.

### Z clips and panel rails

Essentially a commercial version of French cleats, Z clips and panel rails have a lower profile, requiring less room behind the cabinet for installation. They're often made from extruded aluminum, so they can support more weight than French cleats.

## Ganging cabinets together

When the plan calls for wall cabinets adjacent to one another, I like to gang the cabinets together prior to fastening them to the wall. Ganging cabinets is simply securing adjacent cabinets together. This technique helps to maintain a flat face along a run of cabinets, whether or not the wall is flat. Ganging reduces gaps and results in a more professional-looking installation. Plus, ganging produces a cabinet assembly that is stronger and more secure than a single cabinet would be on its own.

Two to three cabinets is about the maximum amount I'll gang together at one time. Any more than that just gets unwieldy and tough to maneuver. I treat ganged cabinets as one big box and install them as a single assembly. The result will be a flatter run with a more seamless look.

## Installing blocking

Anchoring cabinets to a strong support is critical, not only for a professional-looking installation but also for safety. You don't want a cabinet full of dishes to come crashing down.

Most of the time, cabinets are attached to the studs that make up the wall framing, and this provides plenty of strength to secure them. Occasionally, you may need to install a narrow cabinet that falls between the standard 16-in. stud spacing. If this is the case, you need to install blocking behind the cabinet.

Blocking in its most basic form is just a section of 2x4 construction lumber cut to fit between the wall studs. You'll need to cut out a section of drywall to provide some access to install the blocking, which is then nailed or screwed between studs.

Blocking should be positioned behind the nailing strips of the cabinet. For most 30-in.-high wall cabinets, this means installing one section of blocking just above the 54-in. mark. A second piece of blocking is installed just below the 84-in. horizontal mark to secure the upper nailer. Once the blocking is in place, you can reinstall the drywall you cut out earlier and patch it back in place.

**Installing 2x4 block behind the nailers provides strong support for a cabinet that falls between studs.**

Ledgers are simply straight pieces of lumber or plywood. This one is a remnant from building the cabinets. Ledgers should be a little longer than the run's width, to allow for side-to-side adjustments.

# Supporting cabinets

Most of the time I work alone, so I've developed techniques that make large, heavy jobs that usually require more than one person easy to manage on my own. One of those techniques is employing ledgers to support and position wall cabinets during installation.

## Ledgers

Ledgers are nothing more than long, thin, straight pieces of wood. I use scraps of plywood left over from building cabinets, but 2x4s or firing strips work as well. Select a ledger that is a little longer than the distance between vertical layout lines for the cabinet(s) you're going to install. While ledgers work 90 percent of the time, there will be occasions where screwing a ledger to the wall isn't an option, for example, when the room is painted or tiled.

## T-support

A T-support is just two pieces of lumber screwed together in the configuration of a capital T. The support should be about a foot longer than the wall-cabinet installation height. This will allow you to angle the support between the wall and floor, while holding the bottom in place with your foot or a nail into the floor.

## I-beam support

Usually constructed from plywood, I-beam supports are generally 54 in. long. Along with shimming from underneath, these will position the wall cabinets at the right height for installation. For installers who prefer to put base units in first, 19½-in. versions can be made to rest on top of base cabinets.

## Commercial supports

Geared toward professional installers, these vary tremendously in design and price. Some take the form of large jack stands, combining ledgers with their own adjustable supports. Others work like miniature forklifts, allowing you to raise and lower the cabinets into place by just turning a crank.

## workSmart

Laying out fastener locations and drilling pilot holes through the back of the cabinet rather than from the inside eliminate both math and errors in placement.

# Laying out fasteners

**B**egin by placing the wall cabinets in front of their respective locations. It will help you stay organized as you transfer measurements.

1. **Measure the distance** from the layout lines you drew to represent the cabinet sides to the stud center lines.

2. **Transfer the measurements** to the back of the cabinet's upper and lower nailer strips. I place a tick mark mid-height on the nailer.

3. **Drill pilot holes** through the nailer and into the cabinet. The pilot hole should be just a hair smaller than the fastener threads.

4. **Locate the holes** on the inside of the cabinet back. You can clearly see where the fasteners need to be positioned so they'll drive right into the studs. Begin screwing in the installation screws so you won't be fumbling with fasteners when the cabinet is up against the wall, ready for installation.

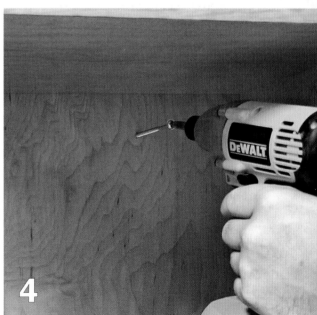

# Ganging Euro-style cabinets

**G**anging cabinets helps to ensure the cabinet fronts are all in alignment and there are no gaps. Securing cabinets to one another also increases the structural integrity of the entire run. (For information on ganging face-frame cabinets, see pp. 52–53.)

1. **Rest the cabinets on a flat surface** and bring their front faces together into the same plane.

2. **Clamp the cabinets together on the front,** top, and bottom.

3. **Clamp the cabinets at the back.**

4. **Drill and countersink for screws** to hold them in place. For Euro-style cabinets, I use 1¼-in. screws to fasten the sides together. For a more finished look, you can use panel connectors (see below).

5. **Drive screws** to join the cabinets.

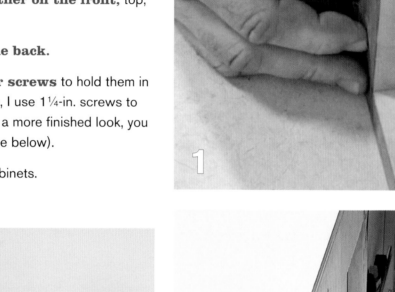

Panel connectors consist of a male and female machine screw. The large head of the connector covers the hole in the cabinet, providing a more finished look.

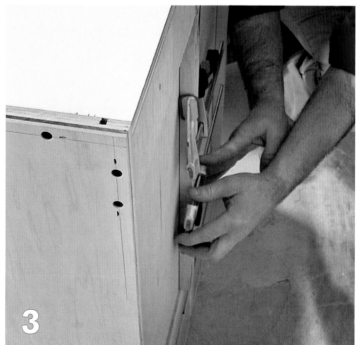

## Ganging face-frame cabinets

When ganging traditional cabinets, use fasteners long enough to pass through one frame and well into the next. This could mean using a 3-in.- to 4-in.-long screw. Also, you'll want to fill the void at the back of the cabinet with shims.

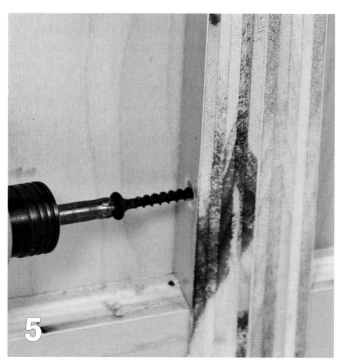

# Installing ledgers

**W**hen you're working alone, ledgers are the simplest and least expensive way to support cabinets during installation.

1. **Position the ledger** on the wall below but just touching the horizontal reference line.

2. **Start at one end,** and work your way along to the other while you secure it to the studs.

3. **Verify the ledger is level** along the way by using a builder's level.

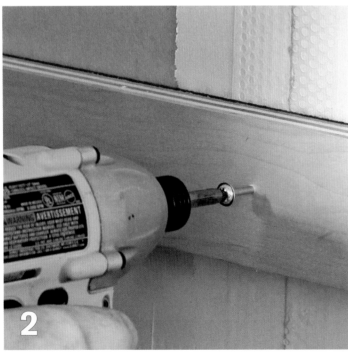

# Installing wall cabinets

**W**ith the ledger firmly in place, you're finally ready to begin hanging your wall cabinets.

1. **Lift the cabinet assembly** onto the ledger and against the wall. An extra pair of hands helps here.

2. **Bump the ganged assembly side to side** until it lines up with the corresponding vertical references.

3. **Starting at one end, check for plumb** and, if needed, shim the cabinet out at the top. If the bottom needs shimming, hold off for now.

(continued on p. 44)

## workSmart

Cabinets above stoves or cooktops can be exposed to lots of heat. Make sure there's a minimum of 30-in. clearance between heat sources and cabinets. Double-check the clearance with your local building inspector.

**4. Drive an upper installation screw** about 90 percent of the way to hold the assembly in place. You're not done yet, but you should be able to let go and step back to admire the start of your cabinet job. Install shims at the stud locations as necessary, and drive the upper installation screws tighter, while checking the face of the assembly for plumb and flatness along the run. Continue driving all the installation screws, including the first one, until they seat. If any screws install with little or no resistance, they've likely missed a stud. You'll want to double-check your layout, and reinstall the screws so they hold.

**5. Remove the support ledger** after all the upper screws are seated.

**6. Use a level to check plumb,** and make sure the face of the run stays flat along its width while you install shims.

**7. Tighten all the lower screws.** Then score the shims where they meet the cabinet and break them off (see p. 57).

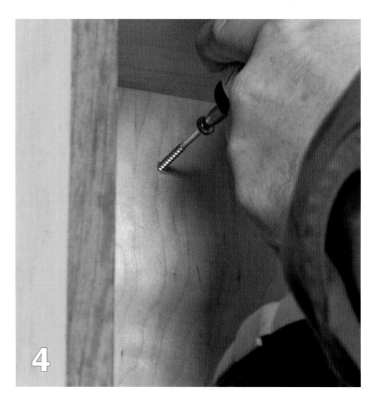

## workSmart

Don't worry about the cabinets being completely tight to the wall along their run. It's much more important to focus on keeping the run flat. As long as the contact points at the studs are shimmed and tight, you're in good shape. You can cover the gap later with a small piece of trim.

chapter

# 5

# Installing base cabinets

**B**ase cabinets are larger and heavier than wall cabinets. Because you're installing them on the floor, you're not fighting gravity during the process, so moving cabinets tends to be easier. On the other hand, you'll usually have some utilities to contend with while setting base units, so you'll have to make some cutouts to provide access to them.

In this chapter, I'll show you how to install base cabinets. I'll address common concerns such as laying out and cutting access holes for electrical boxes and plumbing and how to cut these holes without damaging the cabinets. You'll also learn some techniques for installing free-standing islands and peninsulas.

## Installation strategy

Depending on your layout, base cabinet installation begins in a corner or at the start of a free run of cabinets. Transfer the stud locations to the back of the cabinet, just as for wall cabinets. However, you can't access the bottom of base cabinets to shim them against the wall, so I only put fasteners in the upper nailer. The weight of the cabinets, plus the added rigidity from ganging the cabinets, helps keep everything in place.

Continue the installation by standing the cabinet against the wall and shimming it up to the horizontal

Lay out the fasteners for the base cabinets the same as you did for the wall cabinets. Measure the distance between layout lines and wall studs, and transfer those measurements to the nailer strip on the cabinet.

reference line. This is usually done with standard cedar shims; however, some cabinets may have Euro-levelers (see the sidebar on p. 48). Once aligned, double-check for plumb and square using a spirit level, and make adjustments as needed.

If you're working in a corner, it will be almost impossible to place shims under the rear corner of the toe kick.

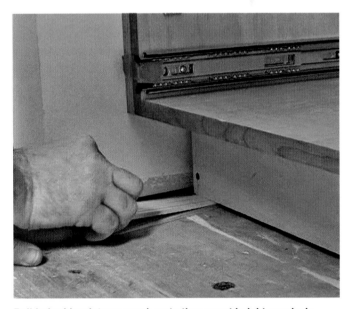

Builder's shims let you sneak up to the correct height, precisely positioning the cabinet plumb and level. For fine adjustments, tap on the end rather than trying to slide the shim.

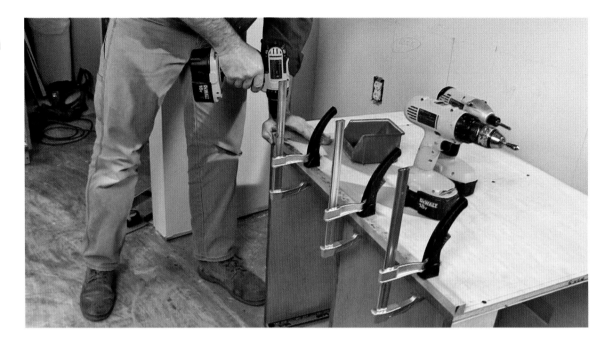

If you need trim support strips to anchor trim that will cover gaps, install them before you permanently attach the cabinets.

## Euro-style cabinet levelers

Cabinets with Euro-style levelers don't require shims to adjust their height, or for plumb or level. Just turn the adjusters to line the cabinet up with reference lines. The weight of the cabinet locks the adjusters, keeping them securely in place.

To adjust the height, install a screw into the bottom of the toe kick (or support). Raising and lowering the screw will allow you to adjust the height of the corner. You may have to position and remove the cabinet a few times to get it just right.

You may need trim supports where there are gaps between walls and cabinets or between cabinets. Later, you will use these strips to anchor the trim. Install trim strips before securing cabinets to the studs.

Once the cabinet is properly positioned, attach it to the wall using 3-in.-long steel cabinet-installation screws. Don't cinch them down supertight against the wall if there's a gap behind the cabinet caused by an irregular wall. Just use a couple shims to fill gaps behind the cabinet. The goal here is to secure the cabinet, not to get it perfectly flat against a wall that's uneven or out of plumb.

Continue the run by transferring the stud locations to the next cabinet, drilling pilot holes, and starting the installation screws. Then line up the cabinet to the front edge of the adjacent installed cabinet. Use a few shims to get the cabinet or face-frame fronts in the same plane, then secure them together with a few clamps. This process is just like ganging wall cabinets to achieve a flat face on the run. Lock the cabinets together permanently with a few screws through the cabinet side or through the face frame on traditional cabinets.

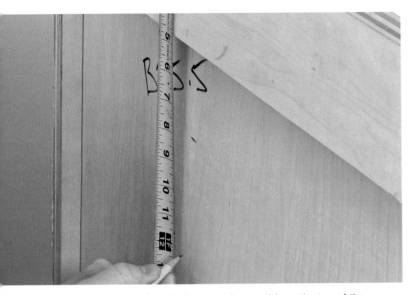

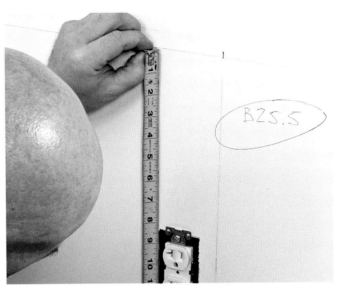

Measurements for utilities are referenced from the top of the cabinet, which will always be positioned at the 34½-in. horizontal reference line. Measure down to find your utility location.

Measure the height of the utility on the wall in relation to the horizontal reference line.

## Dealing with utilities

When a cabinet is being placed around plumbing, such as a sink base, or being placed in front of an electrical outlet, you'll need to modify the cabinet to allow access to utilities.

Begin by laying out where to place the access hole. You'll want to make sure it lines up accurately, or you'll end up with large, unsightly holes in the cabinet back. Transfer the dimensions from the wall to the back of the cabinet. Always measure down from the 34½-in.-high horizontal reference line to the pipe or outlet, rather than up from the floor. The final cabinet height will remain constant, but the floor may vary from low to high, depending on where the cabinet will sit.

Often, plumbing supply pipes will come up through the floor, instead of through a wall. Laying them out is the same. In this case, measure from the wall to the center of the supply pipe, and transfer this distance to the bottom of the cabinet. Repeat the process for each pipe.

For square access holes, such as for outlets, drill a couple of pilot holes large enough for sawblade clearance, and cut out the opening using a jigsaw. For round holes to accommodate plumbing and pipes, a hole saw chucked in a drill gives the best results. You may get a

To cut out a square opening for utility access, use a drill to cut pilot holes in the corners. Then use a jigsaw to finish the cutout. For round holes, use a hole saw slightly larger than the pipe.

When you have utilities to contend with on adjacent faces of the cabinet, such as the supply plumbing and drain in this sink base, oversized access holes will make installation easier. The gaps can be covered with trim escutcheons.

The outlet positioned in the center of this cabinet's back is accessible and will comply with most building codes.

little tearout, but don't worry. The access holes will be covered with trim plates or escutcheons.

If the cabinet has access holes in both the back and the bottom, common in sink base cabinets, cut the holes

## workSmart

Building inspectors are there to help and make sure your project doesn't pose a safety hazard for your home and family. Be sure to check with your local building inspector to familiarize yourself with codes in your area and how they may apply to your project.

a little larger than needed. This will give you extra room to position and angle the cabinet as you install it.

Setting a sink base cabinet in place can be done by one person, but a second set of hands makes it a little easier. Lower the cabinet down on top of the water supply pipes and then up against the wall so that the drain stub passes through the back. Keep in mind that the drain may not pass through perfectly until the cabinet is shimmed up to the horizontal reference. Most building codes prohibit you from covering any type of electrical junction, switch, or outlet, so you need to allow access, even if you'll never use it.

Setting the sink cabinet is best done by two people. Angle the cabinet slightly to place the openings over the drain and the supply pipes.

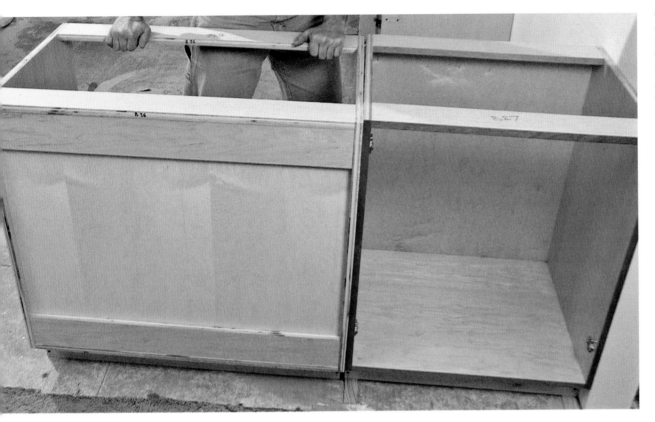

The cabinet at the end of this peninsula needs additional support to keep it in place. Simple 2x4 blocking attached to the floor is a good way to anchor it securely in place.

# Freestanding cabinets

Whether it's a freestanding island or a peninsula that juts out from a wall, cabinets used in these applications have a couple of additional installation concerns. First, you need to position the cabinet and keep it from moving about while in use. You'll also need to consider racking. Because one or more sides of peninsulas and islands are not attached to a wall, the cabinet may be prone to shift from side to side at the top, while the base stays fixed in place. This unwanted movement is called racking.

To anchor the cabinets in place, use 2x4 blocking attached to the floor. Then screw the toe kick to the blocking. A few finish panels applied to the exposed backs of cabinets will not only dress them up but also will help resist any racking forces on the cabinet boxes. Finish panels are covered in more detail in chapter 6.

Blocking doesn't need to be complicated. Here, a 2x4 scrap positioned between layout lines will provide ample surface to lock the peninsula in place.

# Ganging face-frame cabinets

Ganging traditional cabinets is similar to ganging Euro-style cabinets (see pp. 40–41). The main difference is you'll want to install shims or a spacer block to fill the void at the rear of the cabinets.

1. **Clamp the face frames together** at the top and bottom so that the frames are flush to one another.

2. **Drill, countersink, and drive screws** from the inside of one face frame into the other. Make sure you use screws long enough to penetrate deeply into the other face frame.

3. **Use a straightedge** or builder's level across the frames to verify you have a flat run of cabinets while installing the spacer.

4. **Clamp the cabinets at the back** near where you shimmed.

5. **Drill pilot holes, countersink, and drive screws** through the cabinet wall and the shims into the other cabinet.

6. **Use a straightedge** to make sure the face frames are actually flush.

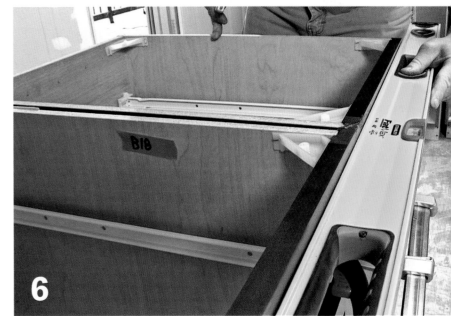

# Installing base cabinets

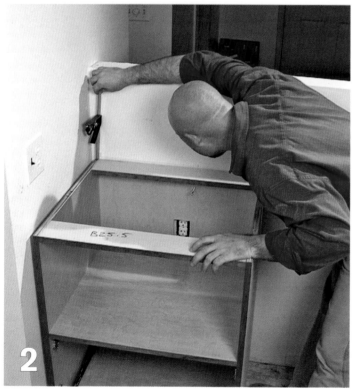

**B**egin in the corner or at an end. Corners are two fixed walls and a definitive point from which to start a run of cabinets. If your design doesn't include a corner, begin at one end of a free run. Base cabinets are anchored to studs just like upper wall cabinets. They weigh twice as much, but because they're resting on the floor, installation is a little easier. Maintaining a level and plumb run is more critical than for wall cabinets because the base cabinets will provide the foundation for the countertop.

1. **Transfer the stud locations** to the back of the cabinet, and mark on the top nailer. Predrill and begin to drive the cabinet-installation screws through the back.

2. **Place the cabinet in position,** and check how far below the corner is from your 34½-in. horizontal reference line to measure how much you'll need to adjust the height.

3. **Raise the inside corner,** if necessary, by driving a screw and adjusting its height until the corner comes up to the horizontal reference line.

4. **Shim the cabinet** until it comes up to level with the reference line.

5. **Double-check that the top is level** using a spirit level. Add additional shims, if necessary.

(continued on p. 56)

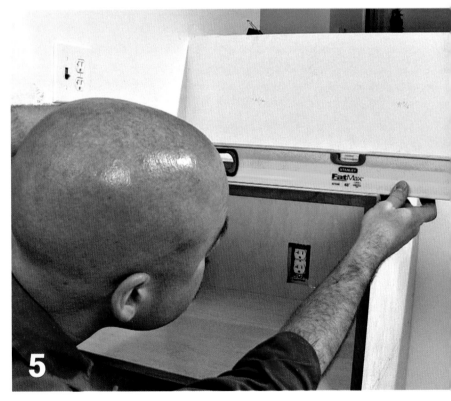

## workSmart

Make all the necessary modifications to the cabinets before permanent installation. Attach any trim support strips you may need. Make any cutouts for electrical and plumbing services, and make sure they are located in the right place.

# Installing base cabinets (continued)

6. **Check using a spirit level from front to back,** and verify it is plumb on adjacent faces.

7. **Drive 3-in. steel cabinet-installation screws** through the back of the cabinet and the top nailer into the wall studs.

8. **Secure the cabinet to adjacent cabinets** using screws or panel connectors through the cabinet side if a Euro-style cabinet, or by attaching the face frames together if a face-frame cabinet (see pp. 52–53).

9. **Fill gaps between the wall and the cabinet** by shimming at the location of the screw through the top nailer. Secure the cabinet to the studs with 3-in.-long steel screws.

10. **Score and snap off the shims.** Use a box cutter to score the cedar shims several times. Then break them off at the score mark.

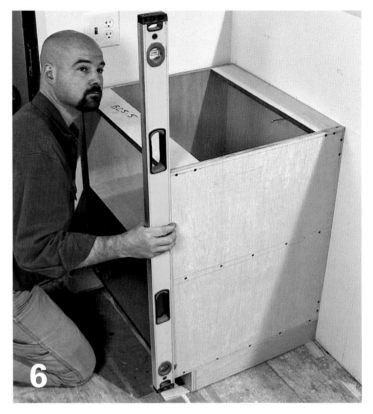

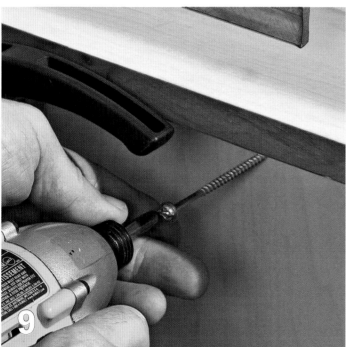

# Making square cutouts for utilities

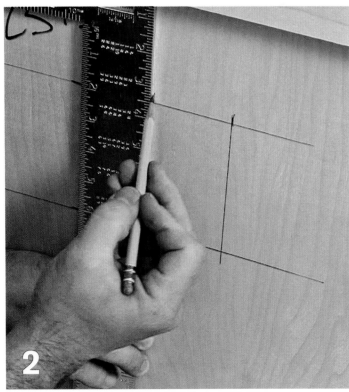

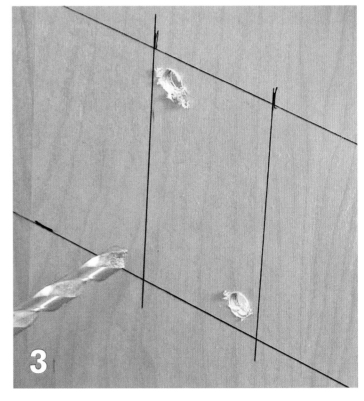

U tilities, such as electrical outlets, water supply lines, and sewage drains are simply a fact of life in a kitchen, and providing access to them is a given. However, getting the cleanest cut hole, positioned accurately, is a way to make your installation look really professional.

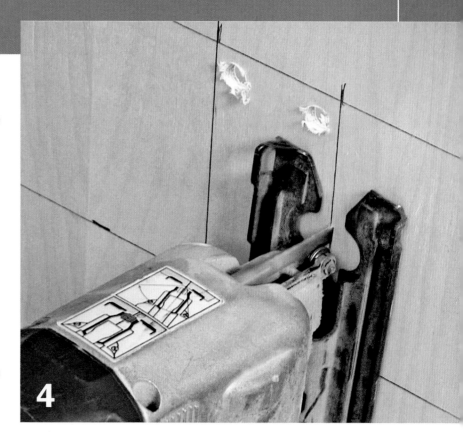

1. **Measure the locations of the utilities on the wall.** Take your measurements from the horizontal reference line and the cabinet layout lines, not from the floor. The floor level varies, but the cabinet height is fixed. To position the top of the cutout, measure down from the top of the cabinet.

2. **Transfer the measurements** to the back or bottom of the cabinet.

3. **Drill starter holes** large enough for a jigsaw blade to pass through.

4. **Complete the cutouts using a jigsaw** with a fine blade to follow the perimeter. Start from the access holes and cut out to the marks.

5. **Clean up the corners** to square up the cutout, and sand away any tearout.

## workSmart

To reduce tearout, apply painter's tape to the surface being cut. The tape not only adds a little extra strength to the wood fibers but also protects the surface of the wood from inadvertent scratches from tool contact. You can also place a scrap of wood on the reverse side of where you're drilling to avoid tearout where the drill will break through.

# Making round cutouts for utilities

**M**aking cutouts for round utilities such as drain and supply pipes is actually easier than making square cutouts because you can use a hole saw. Use a saw slightly larger than the pipe so that you have some room to maneuver the cabinet when placing it.

1. **Measure the distance from the wall** to the center of the pipe. (For holes through the back, measure down from the horizontal reference line to the center.) Measure the distance from each side using the cabinet-placement layout lines.

2. **Transfer the measurements** to the bottom of the cabinet. Don't forget that the thickness of the toe kick/support needs to be considered in your layout.

3. **Mark the center.** While square holes should have the perimeter defined, round holes only require indicating centers.

4. **Drill from the bottom,** cutting the hole a little more than halfway through. Cutting the hole in two steps will avoid tearout.

5. **Complete the hole** by cutting from the inside of the cabinet.

6. **Position the cabinet,** carefully angling it to clear the pipes. After shimming the cabinet to height and leveling it, the holes should line up perfectly. Later, you can add escutcheons or trim plates to conceal the gap around the pipes.

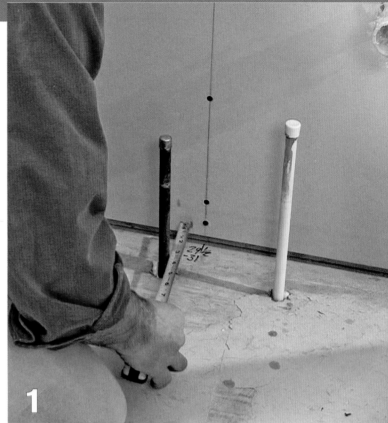

**2**

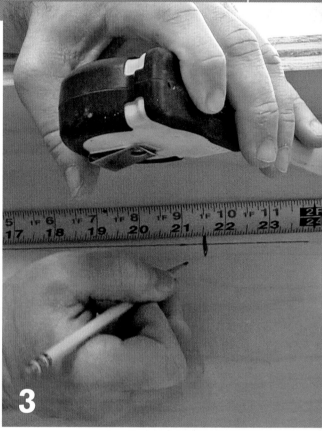

**3**

**5**

**6**

# Installing freestanding cabinets

Freestanding cabinets, such as islands, have no walls to prevent them from shifting. Even a peninsula needs to be secured at the end farthest from the wall to prevent movement and racking. The simplest solution is to attach blocking to the floor and screw through the toe kick to secure the cabinet.

1. **Begin by positioning the cabinets** in their final locations, using your layout lines as reference. Then trace the perimeter of the cabinets at the floor.

2. **Remove the cabinet** and carefully measure back an amount equal to the thickness of the toe-kick support.

3. **Draw the lines intersecting these points.** The new lines will represent where to put blocking to secure the cabinets in position.

4. **Secure lengths of common 2x4** stud lumber to the floor just inside the layout lines representing the inside of the toe kick.

5. **Lower the cabinet over the blocking,** then shim the cabinet level to adjacent cabinet tops and faces.

6. **Drive screws through the toe kick into the blocking** to anchor the cabinet.

**workSmart**

If the peninsula or island is made up of multiple cabinets, gang them together for increased rigidity.

# Installing trim

O nce the base cabinets are installed, your kitchen project really begins to take shape. It may be tempting to throw the doors and drawers back into place, but it's a better idea to install the trim while the cabinets are still bare. That way, there's less risk of damaging any of the finished surfaces.

Trim covers gaps in between cabinets and walls, as well as exposed cabinet sides and bottoms. Plus, trim such as cornice or crown molding can change the style of the project, giving it a more traditional look better suited to an old house or period-style home.

In this chapter, I'll show you a few ways to conceal the construction and installation details of the cabinets. You'll also learn how to provide a solid foundation for trim, even if the cabinet doesn't come that way from the factory. And you'll see how employing some of these methods can transform a group of modular cabinets into a kitchen that looks like it was built in place.

A piece of solid wood or plywood installed where there is a gap between cabinets provides a secure foundation to anchor trim.

## Trim flanges

Traditional cabinets have a face frame that surrounds and extends beyond the cabinet's door, leaving ample surface to attach trim. Euro-style cabinets generally have doors and drawers that extend close to the edges of the cabinets, so there's virtually no surface to mount trim. In that case, the solution is to install trim flanges.

A trim flange is a projected surface used for attaching a trim element. The trim flanges I use are lengths of ¾-in.-thick wood of the same species as the cabinet faces or doors. The flanges range from ¾ in. to 2 in. wide, depending on the size of the trim you'll attach to them.

There are many uses for trim flanges. I use them on the sides of cabinets so I can attach scribed boards to achieve a perfect fit. When I need to support crown molding or cornice molding, I'll install them on the top of the

Traditional cabinets (left) have a generous face frame surrounding the doors and drawers, providing ample room to attach moldings and trim. Euro-style, frameless cabinets (right) don't really provide surface area to attach trim wood. Trim flanges need to be added to support moldings and scribed boards.

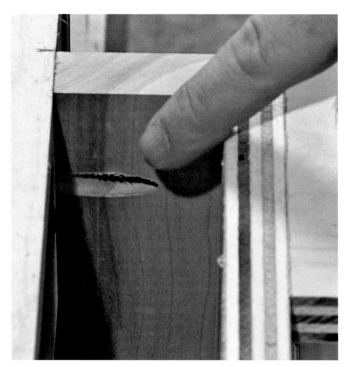

Pocket holes provide a quick method to attach a wider trim flange inconspicuously, as you might need to conceal a wide gap or to support crown molding.

upper cabinets. Or sometimes I place them underneath an upper cabinet to create a little shadow or to hide under-cabinet lighting.

### Installing trim flanges

You can attach trim flanges to cabinets in a number of ways. The easiest is to drill along from inside the front edge of the cabinet. Then drive fasteners from inside the cabinet and into the flange. Just measure the length of the cabinet, cut the trim flange accordingly, and fasten it to the cabinet. You can also drive the screws from the outside edge of the flange, which hides them. Another way to conceal fasteners is by drilling pocket holes. Using a simple pocket-hole jig, you can quickly drill a series of holes along the length of the flange. The screw heads seat below the surface and are invisible from the outside.

Sometimes, it's easier to install a trim flange after the cabinets are secured to the wall, which is usually the case for installing crown molding or under-cabinet lighting. When installing a flange for a scribe board on the side of a cabinet, you'll want to attach it prior to cabinet installation, while you still have ample room to work.

This run of cabinets butts into a corner wall that's not plumb. To achieve a tight fit, the cabinet was offset 1 in. and a trim flange was attached between the cabinet and wall. Later, a trim board will be scribed to the wall and attached to the flange.

Applying a finish panel to these upper cabinets gives them a more custom look. The panel is just like a door but without hinges or other hardware.

## Side treatments

Some cabinet sides have exposed fasteners that need to be covered. Other cabinet sides are bland, usually just covered with paper or vinyl veneer to conceal any screws or staples. In that case, you may want to dress up the sides.

You should plan any side treatments during the design process. One of the most common side treatments is a finish panel, which is typically nothing more than a door that hasn't been drilled for hinges. You can usually order finish panels through the home center or cabinet shop where you purchased your cabinets. In specifying the order, make sure the panel fits flush, not only against the cabinet but also against the wall. If your walls are perfectly flat and plumb, you can just screw the panel in place. But if your walls are wavy or irregular, you'll end up with gaps between the panel and wall. You can fill small gaps with painter's caulk. For larger gaps, you can apply a small molding to conceal it, or you could scribe the back edge of the panel to the wall.

A plywood slab veneered in the same species and finished the same way as the cabinet doors and drawers makes a simple and effective side treatment for a contemporary-style cabinet.

Glue on a strip of hardwood, and trim it flush using a handplane.

Using heat-sensitive edge-banding is an easy way to cover up the raw edges of plywood. The preapplied glue is melted with a household iron, burnished with a block of wood, then trimmed flush.

The side of this painted-cabinet island looks like it's frame and panel, but it's really just square stock applied to the perimeter of the cabinet side.

A simple way to cover the side of a cabinet is to attach a slab of ¾-in.-thick plywood veneered with the same species. This is a great solution if you've built your own cabinets. Use the same finish as you used for the cabinet's primary woods.

You'll also want to conceal the laminations that are exposed on raw plywood edges. These can be covered with veneer tape of the same species. Iron on the tape and trim it flush. The plywood slab will look like a solid piece of wood. For a little more durability, you can glue solid wood to the edge, and trim it flush using a router outfitted with a flush trimming bit or a handplane.

If you're working with face-frame cabinets, which have a reveal between the frame and the cabinet outer face, you can use ¼-in.-thick plywood to cover the side of the cabinet box. Generally, the reveal from the face frame will cover the raw edge of the plywood.

Yet another solution is to apply molding around the perimeter. The result is a faux-finish panel and a custom look. This works best if the cabinet sides are painted, stained, or colored the same species as the fronts. Molding can cover screw holes or assembly fasteners and can really dress up the side of an otherwise bland cabinet box. You could also use square stock around the perimeter instead of profiled molding as shown in the bottom photo at left.

## Under wall cabinets

You may be able to see exposed plywood edging as well as seams or gaps between cabinets when you look up under the upper cabinets. For some people, this area is out of sight, out of mind, and just left as is. For others, the under cabinet is an area where the details make the difference. An easy way to conceal the gaps and raw plywood is to cover the bottom of the run with ¼-in.-thick plywood veneered with the same species as the doors or primary wood of the cabinets.

I especially like to use this technique with traditional cabinetry, where the face frame conceals the edge of the plywood. Cut the plywood to fit between the wall and the trim flanges or face frames. This usually ends up being close to a depth of 11 in. Then attach the plywood skin to the bottom of the cabinets with fast-setting construction adhesive. You can also use a few finish nails or brads to hold it in place. Be sure to use nails that won't penetrate through the bottom of the cabinet into the interior. When working with frameless cabinets, I install a small trim flange along the bottom perimeter. The flange hides the plywood edges just as a face frame would.

A trim flange screwed to the bottom edge of a wall cabinet forms a curtain to conceal under-cabinet lighting, as well as hides the raw edges of the plywood on the bottom of the cabinets.

## Base cabinets

Like wall cabinets, base cabinets may have exposed sides that need to be concealed. Trimming the sides of the base cabinets follows the same process as trimming the sides of upper cabinets.

If you have an island or peninsula in your kitchen, you may also need to cover the back side of the cabinets to conceal nailers or other construction elements. Finish panels or plywood slabs are your best solution.

Cabinets that are only attached to blocking at the floor are more prone to racking or side-to-side movement. Adding panels to the back not only dresses up the island or peninsula but also makes it stronger by helping the cabinets resist racking stress.

If you choose to cover the back with a slab, then cut the plywood to cover the entire exposed run. This will make the job quicker and more efficient, and it results in

This cabinet's back and side were exposed, so I covered them with finish panels. Note that all the panels on the back are the same size, making it less complicated to match panels with cabinets. They're also the same size as the doors in the surrounding cabinets.

In this kitchen, I used a finish panel at the end of the base run. It will disguise the side of the dishwasher that will be installed later.

Under the base cabinets, the screws and joinery of these toe kicks are visible, making it obvious they are multiple units. A seamless toe kick will make the assembly look more built in.

a stronger back. When using multiple finish panels, I will often gang them together using pocket screws, and hang them as one assembly. Whatever method you use to cover the back side, the panels or slabs are simply screwed in place from the interior of the cabinet. Again, use the longest screws you can without the screw penetrating to the outside.

## Toe kicks

An item specific to base cabinets is the toe kick or cabinet support. Some cabinets have raw plywood supports, which must be covered just to blend in with the cabinets. Other cabinets have completely finished toe kicks, but even with these, you'll usually have gaps between the supports due to face-frame reveal or gaps under the cabinet due to shimming.

A simple way to cover the toe kick is to use off-the-shelf vinyl base molding, available from flooring stores and home centers. This type of molding is flexible, cuts with a razor knife, and provides a smooth transition from the floor to the face of the toe kick. Some versions apply with two-sided tape. Others require an adhesive to hold them in place.

My solution for toe kicks is to use ¼-in.-thick plywood. Just crosscut each piece to length using a miter saw, and secure it to the cabinets with construction adhesive applied to the back. Once the plywood is positioned, a few brads or pin nails will keep it in place while the adhesive dries. Any irregularities between the floor and bottom of the toe-kick trim can be covered with a simple shoe molding or quarter-round.

If your cabinets have Euro-style levelers, you'll have to install thicker kick boards to conceal the open space below the cabinets. Some manufacturers include the components to do this. Others make them available as kits. But installing these are a snap, literally. The kick board is secured to the levelers with little clips that snap on the legs of the levelers.

Installing a trim flange to the top of a cabinet enables you to install a variety of trim components, including soffits and crown and cornice moldings.

## Cabinet tops

I've left the tops of the upper cabinets for last. Not that they're an afterthought, but sometimes they don't need any trim, which makes the installation easier. Left bare, the top of the cabinet can be an area to place decorative containers or other accents or to store items you don't often use.

Sometimes bare upper cabinets are butted against a dropped portion of a ceiling called a soffit. In this situation, you may have small gaps between the tops of the cabinet and the ceiling that need to be concealed. The best way to cover these gaps is to use a small molding, such as a corner-round, in the same manner as you would to cover up a gap between a floor and a toe kick.

If there's room above the cabinets, you can add some visual interest by applying a crown or cornice molding, both to dress them up and to help them blend better

with traditional architecture. Another option is a simple double top, which is basically a couple slabs, or flat trim, offset slightly and placed on top of one another. The double top works well in a Shaker or Arts and Crafts kitchen.

For cabinets that flank a window, a common trim choice is a valance. A valance is nothing more than a board that spans from one cabinet across an open space to another cabinet. The valance can be as simple or as fancy as you want it to be.

I've barely touched on the variety of molding and trim applications you could encounter in a kitchen. The scenarios I've covered are some of the more common ones you'll come across, though. Remember, as long as you have a solid foundation to secure them, you can always add or build up additional moldings to conceal gaps, add decorative elements, or cover raw edges or fasteners.

In this traditional-style kitchen, soffits and crown molding provide a seamless transition from the top of the cabinets to the ceiling.

# Installing a narrow trim flange

I n some cases, you'll attach trim flanges where trim will cover gaps between the wall and the cabinet or between cabinets before the cabinets are installed. For narrow trim flanges, you can use drywall screws to secure the flange.

1. **Measure the gap** you need to cover with trim to determine the width of the stock you'll need.

2. **Cut a piece of hardwood** of the same species to the same length as the cabinet.

3. **Clamp the flange securely** to the cabinet side, then drill and countersink for screws. Drive screws that are long enough to penetrate into the cabinet side but not so long that they come through to the interior of the cabinet.

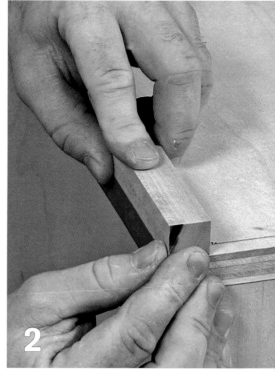

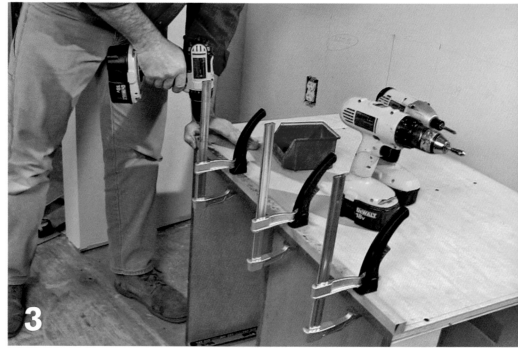

# Installing a
# wide trim flange

Pocket screws provide a quick and secure method for attaching trim flanges to cabinet sides, especially where a wider board is needed to fill a gap.

1. **Set up your pocket-hole jig** to hold the stock securely. Mark off the locations of the pocket screws, and align your marks with the marks on the jig.

2. **Drill the holes** using the pocket-screw step-bit. Drill to the depth of the stop collar. You may need to clear the waste to drill to full depth.

3. **Drive the pocket screws** using the square-tipped driver designed for pocket screws.

1

**Pocket-screwed flanges offer the best solution where there are wide gaps, such as in this situation, where a base cabinet meets a peninsula.**

2

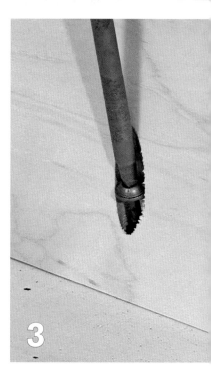

3

# Installing a finish panel

inish panels dress up the sides and backs of raw-sided or bland cabinets. While the specific construction of the cabinets you're working with may vary, the techniques to install finish panels are adaptable to most cabinets.

1. **Position the panel into place.** Install shims or spacers as needed to bring the panel into the same plane as the face frame (if applicable).

2. **Check to make sure the overhang is equal** top to bottom. If there are noticeable gaps to the wall, you may wish to scribe for a tight fit or cover the gap with a small molding.

3. **Rabbet the back edge of the panel** using a table-saw or router mounted with a rabbeting bit. If you need to scribe or make adjustments, it's easier to remove material because the rabbet provides a narrower edge.

4. **Make small adjustments using a block plane.** For more extensive scribing, use a rasp, jigsaw, or bandsaw. Smooth and sand as required for a finished appearance.

5. **Clamp the panel to lock it into position.**

6. **Predrill, countersink, and drive screws** from inside the cabinet. Drill into the frame of the finish panel, not into the inner panel.

## workSmart

When attaching finish panels, be sure to use screws that are long enough to hold the panel in place but not so long that they'll penetrate through to the outside.

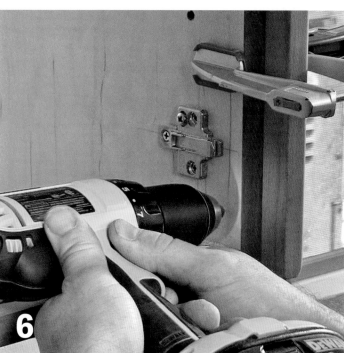

# Installing an applied toe-kick cover

Raw toe kicks not only show exposed edges of plywood and particleboard, but they also have large gaps that were created while shimming the cabinets plumb and level. Covering toe kicks with seamless strips of plywood conceals the construction installation details and makes the cabinets look more like a single built-in unit.

1. **Rip full lengths of finished plywood to width.** Usually, $3\frac{7}{8}$ in. will cover the exposed toe kick while still allowing the trim to be positioned easily.

2. **Cut to length.** Measure the run of bases, and use the longest piece possible for a seamless appearance.

3. **Use quick-setting construction adhesive** along the length of the plywood, focusing the flow around the perimeter, as shown.

4. **Press firmly to get a good bond,** and secure the plywood with pin nails to hold it in place while the adhesive dries.

5. **Conceal the gap at the floor.** Use a small molding such as a quarter-round, which is somewhat flexible and can follow the variations of an uneven floor.

**2**

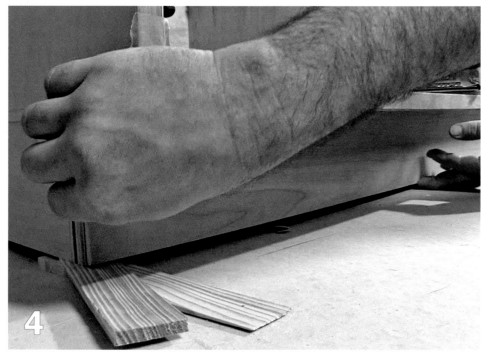

**4**

**5**

# Installing
# countertops

N ow that the cabinets have been installed, it's time to install the countertops. There are many options in counter-top material, ranging from plastic laminate and butcher block to stone, metal, concrete, and solid-surface materials. Some of these materials require special tools and skills and are best left to the pros.

But plastic laminate is durable, economical, and comes in a wide range of colors and patterns. You can buy laminate (post-form) countertops as stock items at home centers and cabinet-supply retailers. Another option is to have the countertop custom fabricated, which will offer you a greater range of choices. Or you can build plastic laminate countertops yourself.

In this chapter, I'll show you how to fabricate a simple laminate countertop, how to prep for countertop installation, and how to cut a counter down to size. Plus, I'll show how to join mitered counters together for L-shaped cabinet layouts. And you'll also learn how to cut out for a sink.

Post-form counters must be shimmed up when used with Euro-style cabinets to provide clearance for drawer and door operation.

## Prepping for countertops

Depending on the countertop type and cabinet style, you may need to shim or add spacers to the top of the cabinets to bring the counter up to the 36-in. height and provide clearance for the doors to open. This is usually the case with post-form counters, especially when used with Euro-style cabinets and full-overlay doors.

Most post-form countertop manufacturers offer "build-up" kits to shim their counters to proper height. Or you can make your own spacers by cutting strips of plywood. Attach the spacers to the cabinet tops with a few brads to provide support for the countertops.

**workSmart**

When ordering your countertops, make sure to plan ahead and include any necessary build-up, corner, or end-cap kits in your purchase.

Cutting a post-form countertop from below helps reduce tearout, resulting in a more professional-looking cut.

To cut post-form countertops, use a fine-multitooth crosscut blade for a handheld circular saw. Blades designed for plywood work well for this purpose.

To ensure a perfect 90-degree cut, use a framing square to lay out the cut line. Use a straightedge to guide your saw.

**workSmart**

To avoid tearout and splitting the laminate, always support the weight of material that will be cut out or cut off.

## Working with post-form countertops

Countertop shops can custom fabricate a post-form countertop to your required length and configuration. But if you're using an off-the-shelf post-form countertop, it will usually have to be cut to size and finished off at the ends. For a professional appearance, you'll want to make a clean cut with little or no tearout. The best way to cut a laminate countertop is from the bottom, using a fine-tooth blade in a circular saw and a straightedge to guide the saw as you cut.

Begin by measuring the length of the countertops. Don't forget to include any overhangs for end-of-run situations. Transfer the measurements to the underside of the countertop. Figure in the offset of the blade, and clamp a straightedge in place to guide the cut. This can be tricky the first time you do it, so practice the technique in the waste area a few times before making the actual cut.

Post-form counters that don't butt up to a wall should have their exposed ends covered with the materials from an end kit. This kit contains a filler block and laminate, precut to match the profile of the counter, as well as the integral backsplash.

## End treatments

To cover the raw edge of the post-form counter, end kits are available that match the color of your counter. These kits vary a little depending on application and manufacturer, but they basically fall into two types. In both cases, the kits are sensitive to right-hand or left-hand orientation, so make sure to order the correctly facing kit for your installation.

The first type of kit covers the raw substrate and is used for end-of-run applications. It contains an L-shaped piece of laminate and generally a filler or spacer block and adhesive. Once all the pieces are glued together, you simply trim the laminate flush and ease the edges for a professional look.

If your countertop butts against a wall, the second type of kit extends the backsplash. These kits usually include a laminate-covered block, with a negative of the counter profile cut into it, as well as adhesive caulk. The block is glued into place after the counter has been installed.

## Joining mitered post-form counters

Many kitchen layouts are L-shaped and have corners, so you may need to deal with a miter joint when installing your post-form counter. Fortunately, countertops with

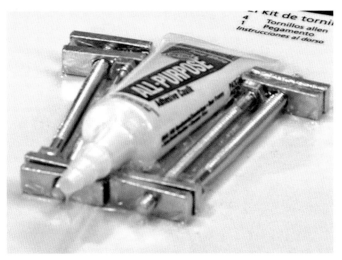

Kits are available for countertops that join at mitered corners. The kit usually includes the adhesive as well as special bolts that fit into recesses in the countertop substrate.

premitered ends that can be joined on site are usually available. In addition to the matching mitered sections, you'll also need a connector kit. The kit contains special bolts that draw the countertops together and adhesive caulk to seal the joint.

Join the counters by applying adhesive caulk along the edges of the miter and aligning the counter sections together. Then install the connector bolts into the factory-cut recesses. Tighten them, checking the joint alignment as you go. Once all the bolts are tightened and the edges are flush, pin the backsplashes together by driving a finish nail into the end of the joint.

Most sink manufacturers supply cutting templates. Align the centerline, and tape the template to the underside of the countertop. Cut the opening using a jigsaw outfitted with a fine-tooth blade.

Depending on the size, shape, or location of the sink, you may need to make modifications to the cabinets. Here, I'll need to cut back the spacers and nailers to accommodate an extra-deep sink.

## Cutting out for sinks

I find it easiest to attach a sink basin and faucet prior to installing the countertop. This practice gives me more room to work and less time spent crawling around inside of a cabinet. The cut is also cleaner, and there's less danger of tearout or chipping the laminate.

Most sinks come with a cutting template or pattern. After you've transferred the centerline of the sink location to the underside of the countertop, align the template with the mark. Tape the pattern to the countertop with masking tape.

Drill a hole at each corner of the template to provide access for a jigsaw blade. Carefully cut along the template lines. Once you've made the rough cut, check your work by inserting the sink into the counter and trim where necessary for a good fit. Then place the countertop on the cabinets to check for any interference where the sink will be located. Depending on the cabinet construction details, you may need to trim the top stretchers and

build-up material. Once again, check your work by setting the sink in place. When you're happy with the fit, remove the countertop and install the sink and faucet as specified by the manufacturer.

### Cutting from above

Cutting the sink opening after the countertop has been installed is trickier. There's a greater possibility of tearout or chipping the laminate. In integral backsplash applications, tool access may be a problem. If the sink is very deep, you may need to use a reciprocating saw or handsaw to make the cut near the backsplash.

One way to minimize tearout is to use masking tape along the cut line. Leave some uncut waste in the corners to support the cutout until you're ready to make the final cuts. And whether cutting from below or above, always support the weight of the cutout until you're ready to remove it.

Countertops are fragile once cut and fitted for a sink. Use extreme caution when moving and maneuvering the countertop until it is secured in place.

## Installing a post-form counter

Gently lift the countertop into position. You may have to roll or rotate it into place, but it will usually slip right in. Then push the countertop firmly against the wall and lock it into place with a few clamps.

From inside the cabinets, drill a series of pilot holes to fasten the countertop. Secure it into place using screws that are long enough to pass through the stretchers and spacers but not so long that they protrude through the top of the counter. I use four screws per cabinet, locating them a few inches in from the sides. Be sure to start in the center of the counter, and work your way to the ends to spread the clamping force of the fasteners evenly.

Wrap up the countertop installation by taking a few moments to inspect all the edges for any sharp spots. If you find a sharp edge, ease it with some 220-grit sandpaper. Then apply caulk as necessary to seal joints, as well as to conceal small gaps.

### Preinstalled brackets

Some stock cabinets use plastic brackets in the corners to attach the countertop. Generally, these brackets have a reinforced hole in their center to locate the fastener.

# Building a laminate countertop

Building a laminate countertop yourself can save you some money. The skills required are fairly basic. You begin by building the substrate from particleboard. Then you cut the laminate, apply glue, and install the laminate. As simple as that!

1. **Determine the correct size of the substrate** by measuring the run of cabinets it will cover, including any overhangs. Rip ¾-in.-thick particleboard to size. Also rip 4-in.-wide strips of particleboard to be used as build-up strips.

2. **Mark the location of the build-up strips,** and spread a generous amount of glue where the build-up strips will be placed.

3. **To secure the build-up strips** to the substrate while the glue dries, use brads or staples long enough to reach through the material. Trim the build-up strips flush with the substrate.

4. **Lay out where you'll cut** to break down the laminate into manageable sheets. Plan your cuts to maximize the use of the material, but remember to allow enough overhang for trimming flush to the substrate.

5. **Cut the laminate to size** using a circular saw out-fitted with a fine cutoff blade. A blade especially designed for laminate is best, but blades meant for cutting plywood will also work. Use a straightedge to guide the saw.

6. **Begin with the edges.** Spread contact cement on both the back of the laminate and the surface to which it will be glued. Allow the contact cement to dry until it is no longer tacky to the touch. Follow the manufacturer's guidelines.

(continued on p. 86)

## warning

Solvent-based contact cement can be extremely volatile and hazardous to your health. Use it in a well-ventilated area, and wear a properly rated ventilator fitted with the correct filters. The solvents in the cement are so powerful they will dissolve foam brushes. If possible, use solvent-resistant brushes and rollers to spread the cement.

# Building a laminate countertop (continued)

7. **Burnish the glued strip** using a wooden block to ensure good adhesion.

8. **Trim the overhang using a laminate trimmer.**

9. **Use a block plane** or sharp chisel to trim the excess in corners and where the router can't reach.

10. **Spread the contact cement** on large, flat surfaces using a roller. Coat both the back of the laminate and the substrate evenly. Allow the cement to dry until it's no longer tacky.

11. **Lay out battens** (strips of wood or dowels) to keep the laminate from contacting the substrate while you position it.

12. **Remove the battens one by one,** working from the center. Use each batten as you remove it to help smooth down the laminate and press out air bubbles.

13. **Roll out the laminate from the center** toward the edges to eliminate bubbles and ensure good adhesion.

14. **Trim the laminate flush to the edge** using a laminate trimmer. I use an integral-pilot bit (without a removable bearing) for this process and a little mineral oil as a lubricant for the pilot.

15. **Ease the junction of the top and the edge** using a fine mill file held at 45 degrees.

# Prepping cabinets for countertop installation

The standard height for countertops is 36 in. from the finished floor height. The industry standard for cabinet height is 34½ in. If the counter you choose to install is less than 1½ in. thick (as is the case with most post-form counters), you'll need to build up the top of the cabinets to make up the difference.

1. **Place the countertop over the cabinets** to get an accurate measurement.

2. **Measure the thickness of the countertop** (build-up material, if any, plus the substrate and laminate). Subtract this from 1½ in. to determine the thickness of the spacers you'll need.

3. **Rip spacers to width and cut to length.** To distribute and support the weight of the countertop, the spacers should be wide enough to span between the front and back edges of the cabinet and the same length as the depth of the run.

4. **Tack the spacers in place.** A few brads or finish nails will keep the spacers from moving around during installation.

## workSmart

Build-up kits are available from most post-form countertop manufacturers. Depending on the length of the cabinet run, several kits may be required.

# Cutting post-form countertops

**W**hen using an off-the-shelf post-form counter-top from a home center, you'll probably need to cut it to the correct size. For a clean, professional result with minimal tearout, you should make your cuts from underneath.

1. **Measure to length and mark the cut line.** Remember to take into account any overhang for end-of-run applications.

2. **Lay out the cut line using a square.** Mark off a second line about 3 in. beyond the final length. Cutting here first will help prevent the waste from snapping off, damaging the good portion of the counter. This cut also provides an opportunity to practice your technique before the final cut.

3. **Clamp a straightedge in place** to guide the saw. Place spacers, if necessary, under the straightedge to bring all the parts of the countertop to the same level. This allows you to make the entire cut in one pass and helps to ensure it's straight.

4. **To cut the backsplash,** rotate the straightedge and saw onto the backsplash. Use spacers, if necessary.

5. **Cover the raw edge** with the materials from an end kit from the manufacturer. Attach the laminate with contact cement applied to both surfaces. Follow the cement manufacturer's instructions. Trim the edges flush using a laminate trimmer.

## workSmart

Unless you're using a cutting guide that aligns on the actual cut line, remember to figure in the offset of the sawblade.

# Joining mitered corners

I n addition to a miter-assembly kit, you'll need wrenches of the proper size, nitrile or latex gloves to keep your hands clean, and lots of paper towels.

1. **Apply a generous bead of adhesive caulk** (supplied in the kit) on the mitered edge. This not only glues the two counters together but also fills the gap between them, making the joint less susceptible to water damage during use.

2. **Align the two countertop sections** at their front edges with the countertop bottom up.

3. **Install the first connector bolt,** making sure that the front edge and the top of the two sections are in the same plane.

4. **Tighten the bolts down the line,** checking as you go that the parts remain in the same plane. When you can't feel the transition between the counters, tighten the bolt down and move on to the next one. Tweak the counter up and down until the edges are flush, tighten each connector bolt, and repeat.

5. **Clean off the excess adhesive** before it dries. Use the solvent recommended by the adhesive manufacturer and paper towels.

6. **Secure the backsplashes** with a finish nail driven through one backsplash and into the other to keep them from moving.

> ## warning
> Some solvents are highly combustible. Lay out solvent-soaked rags or paper towels to dry completely before disposing of them.

# Cutting out for a sink

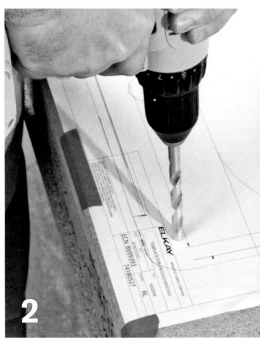

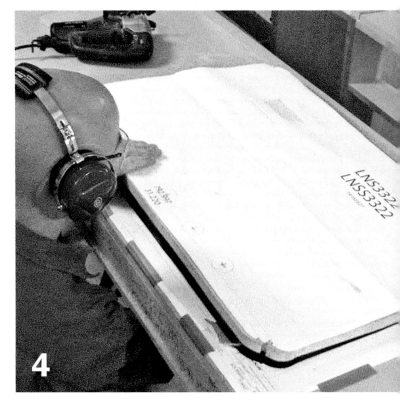

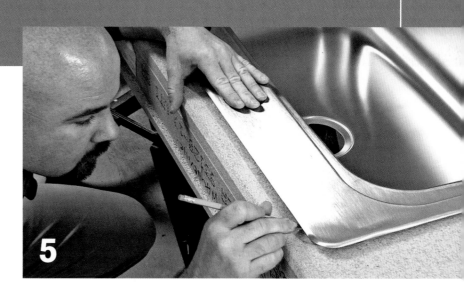

It's much easier to cut out the hole for the sink and install it before the countertop is installed. Cut from the bottom for a more professional result.

1. **Measure to find the centerline for the sink** and align the template. Double check to make sure the sink will actually fit by laying it over the template. This will also give you a preview of any modifications you may need to make to the top of the cabinets. Tape the template to the underside of the countertop.

2. **Drill ⅜-in. access holes** for the jigsaw blade at each corner of the template.

3. **Cut carefully along layout lines** using a jigsaw outfitted with a fine-tooth blade.

4. **Support the waste** as you approach the end of the cut. Place sawhorses beneath the cutout or use strategically placed clamps to secure it. Allowing the waste to fall freely can damage the countertop.

5. **Check your work.** Insert the sink into the counter, and trim where necessary for a good fit. Depending on the size and location of the sink, you may also need to trim the cabinet stretchers and spacers.

6. **Install stainless steel and other light sinks** held by clips according to the manufacturer's instructions. You may also wish to install the faucet at this point. Other types of sinks may need to be installed after the countertop has been secured in place.

7. **Rotate the countertop into place.** Use caution when moving the countertop now, as it will be much weaker until it is secured to the cabinets.

# Installing a countertop

The countertops must align with one another in the same plane. Add shims and spacers as necessary, and make sure all debris is removed from the cabinet tops.

1. **Clamp the countertop to the nailers** to prevent it from shifting as you drill pilot holes for the screws.

2. **Drill pilot holes for the screws** from beneath. I install two screws in the front nailer, locating them a few inches in from the sides.

3. **Drill pilot holes in the back nailer.**

4. **Drive the screws.** From the center of the countertop, work toward the ends to distribute the holding pressure of the screws.

5. **Ease any sharp edges.** Raw laminate can be as sharp as a knife. Using 220-grit sandpaper, lightly sand the edges until they are friendly to the touch. Then apply caulk to fill small gaps and protect the joints from water damage.

**workSmart**

Be sure that you don't drill through the top. A drill stop or a piece of masking tape on the bit will help you gauge how deep to drill. Also, make sure that the screws are long enough to bite into the countertop but not so long that they'll poke through the top.

# Installing hardware

**Shelves supported by removable metal pins can be adjusted to suit virtually any storage need.**

Your cabinet installation is in the home stretch. The only things left to do are to reinstall all of the drawers, pullouts, and doors, and add the hardware to make your cabinets fully functional.

In this chapter, I'll show you how to reinstall and fine-tune all of the components you removed earlier to make the cabinets lighter. You'll learn how to adjust Euro-style hinges and undermount drawer slides. Plus, you'll see how to install the decorative hardware to make the cabinet components fully functional.

## Reinstalling interior components

Start reinstalling components by working from the inside of the cabinet to the outside. The simplest items to put back in place are basic shelves. Metal shelf-support pins keep them level and ready for use, as well as allow height adjustments.

Pullouts and drawers are the next items to be reinstalled. The simplest drawers use white epoxy slides, also known as Euroslides. Simply tip one into the other to reinstall the drawer or pullout.

Metal side-mount slides are also pretty simple, but make sure they line up smoothly. It's easy to get these misaligned and damage their inner workings. Push the runners all the way into the cabinet, then line up the drawer portion with the case portion. Next, push the drawer all the way into the cabinet. When the drawer

is reassembled, the initial closing force may be a little greater, but subsequent operation should be smooth and effortless. If it's difficult to close the drawer on reassembly or if you hear crunching noises, something's not lined up right. Remove the drawer and check the installation.

For undermount slides, begin with the slides extended from the cabinet. Lay the drawer box on top of the metal runners, then just push the drawer box into the cabinet. The runners engage the front retaining clips automatically, securing the drawer in place. You can make adjustments to this type of slide by tilting it at the back to get an even and level slide operation.

**Euroslides just slip into one another. Drop the drawer wheel behind the cabinet wheel, and push the drawer past its detent to reinstall.**

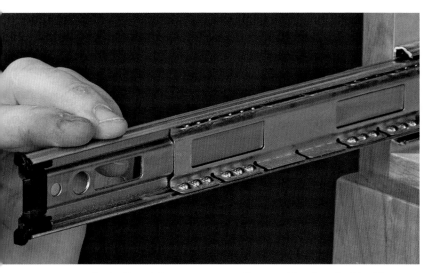

A misaligned drawer can cause the caged bearings in this side-mount slide to be damaged. If you encounter binding on reinstallation, remove the drawer and inspect the slide for distorted guides.

Drawers designed for undermount slides are placed on the runners and then pushed into place. The latching mechanism will automatically secure the drawer once it's pushed into the cabinet.

## Check the web for specific hardware information

It's possible that your cabinets may have a different type of hinge or runner system than shown here. To provide specific information about their products, most manufacturers have resources and answers to FAQs (frequently asked questions) on their websites. These sites can address many of your questions and may also provide helpful illustrations and installation instructions.

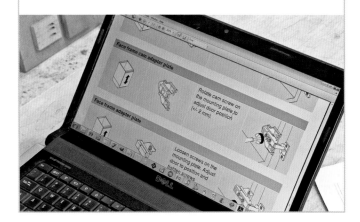

# Reinstalling and adjusting doors

To reinstall the doors on most Euro-style frameless cabinets, just align the front of the hinge with the front of the mounting plate and click the hinge into place. Not every Euro-style hinge has a clip attachment. Your hinges may have a screw at the back edge to secure it to the base plate. In this case, the screw also acts as the depth adjuster for the door.

Most European hinges are adjustable in two or three dimensions. They can move in and out, up and down, and side to side. You can combine adjustments to twist or rotate a door as well, making it easy to achieve the perfect fit. Just remember, some of the fasteners on European hinges may have Pozidriv heads, so be sure to use the correct driver to avoid rounding them out (see p. 29).

## Other types of doors

When working with traditional face-frame cabinetry, there are two types of hinges you'll encounter: a modified Euro-style cup hinge and a barrel-style hinge.

Face-frame-mounted, Euro-style hinges are usually fastened onto the face frame, where they can be adjusted up and down. Premium face-frame cup hinges allow multiaxis adjustment. Premium hinges typically have a

To achieve an even reveal at the edge of a cabinet, as well as an even gap between doors, adjust Euro-style hinge arms in tandem.

Most Euro-style hinges designed for face frames attach with a single screw that allows some vertical adjustment.

few small screws surrounding the larger one that fastens it to the cabinet. Like frameless Euro-style types, premium hinges offer six-way adjustment.

Another common hinge is the barrel-type hinge, which is simply fastened to the face frame. Some may have slotted screw holes, which offer limited vertical adjustment, while many others are just fixed in place.

## Knobs and pulls

The biggest challenge in installing knobs and pulls is to locate them consistently. To accomplish this easily, you can use a simple jig for laying out the fastener location. You can buy hardware-installation jigs at most home centers, or you can make your own from scrap plywood.

Once the fastener locations are marked, drill the corresponding holes, then just screw the fastener and the pull together. When installing decorative hardware on drawers, you may need to replace the fasteners that came with your hardware, utilizing a screw that is long enough to pass through the drawer box as well as the applied drawer front. Adjustable-length screws are available that allow you to snap the screw to the correct length. Make sure the thread pitch matches your hardware.

Jigs help you locate knobs and pulls for a uniform and consistent appearance. The jig at left is shopmade. The one at right was purchased at a home center.

Fasteners that come packaged with hardware may not be long enough for all applications. Be sure to use screws that will hold knobs and pulls securely, and make sure the thread pitch is the same on the replacement fasteners.

# Adjusting undermount slides

**E**uro-style slides are simple to install but don't offer much in the way of adjustability. Likewise, most side-mounted metal slides don't adjust either, although a few models may offer some up-and-down movement. Undermount slides, on the other hand, offer ways not only to raise the drawer box but also to tilt the assembly from front to rear, as well as from side to side. You can both level the drawer box and make adjustments to improve drawer operation.

1. **Reinstall the drawer box.** Lower the drawer box on the fully extended runners, then push the drawer into the cabinet until the front locking mechanisms engage.

2. **Adjust the tilt of the drawer.** Moving levers at the rear of the drawer will tilt the drawer in and out at the top. The front of the drawer should be level and in the same plane as the front of the cabinet.

3. **Adjust the height of the drawer.** The gray sliders (at the top of the photo) on the locking mechanisms will raise and lower the drawer front independently on each side. This also allows correction of drawers that are crooked. Complete the adjustment by operating the drawer several times to verify alignment.

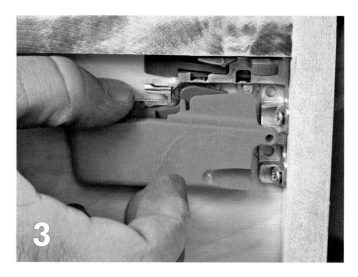

# Adjusting Euro-style hinges

**E**uro-style hinges allow for adjustment in several directions. Many Euro-style hinges have screws with Pozidriv heads, so be sure to use the proper driver.

1. **Secure the hinge to the mounting plate.** Hinges either clip on or screw on to the mounting plate.

2. **Adjust the hinge protrusion** using the rear-most screw. Aim for a ⅛-in. gap between the closed door and the cabinet face. The door can be adjusted in and out by adjusting both hinges at the same time. A warped door can sometimes be corrected by adjusting protrusion in opposite directions at the top and bottom of the door.

3. **Adjust the door height.** Most Euro-style hinges have a screw to accomplish this on the mounting plate. Try for even gaps at the top and bottom of each door. Focus more on the hinge side of the door. Gaps on the unhinged side will be magnified, even with small adjustments.

3A. **Adjust the door height.** Some Euro-style hinges, especially those used on face frames, don't have height-adjustment screws on the hinge or plate. In that case, loosen the mounting plate from the cabinet and move it up or down.

4. **Remedy crooked doors.** Making side-to-side adjustments independently on each hinge can help turn a skewed door into a plumb door. On some hinges, this screw is concealed within the hinge body.

5. **Adjust the doors from side to side.** The goal is to create uniform gaps between doors on each cabinet and on adjacent cabinets, so the entire project shares the same clearances.

# Installing knobs and pulls

The last step of the installation is mounting the decorative hardware to the cabinet doors and drawers. The goal is consistent alignment, and jigs help achieve it.

1. **Measure the hardware** to determine the distance of the fastener holes from one another (in the case of pulls). Determine how far from the edge of the door or drawer front the hardware will be. Transfer the measurements to the drawer or door front.

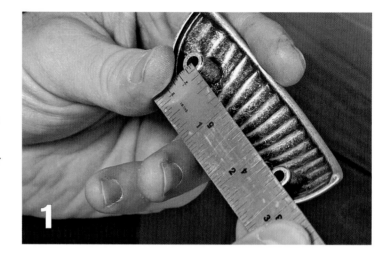

1A. **Or use a jig** to determine the location of the hardware. Transfer layout marks using a pencil. Choose the appropriate center-to-center distance that applies to your hardware.

2. **Create a dimple to position the drill.** Use a punch or awl to create a positive indentation to start drilling and keep the drill bit from wandering.

3. **Drill for the hardware screws.** To minimize tearout, drill from the front using a standard twist bit. Generally, a 3/16-in. bit will provide the proper clearance for the fastener. Using a backer block on the rear of the drawer will minimize tearout where the bit exits.

4. **Insert the screws** through the rear of the drawer or door. Make sure they are the correct length to penetrate both the drawer box and the applied front.

5. **Tighten the screws to secure the pull** or knob. Don't overtighten or you may strip the threads in the hardware.

1A

3

5

## Make your own drilling jig

**U**niversal hardware-locating jigs are available at most home centers. But you can easily make your own alignment jigs. A few pieces of scrap plywood can be joined together to make a jig that will not only consistently position your hardware but will also guide the drill bit.

To make a simple jig for installing cabinet knobs, cut a piece of ½-in. plywood to the same width as the stile of the door (the upright member of the door frame). Attach 1-in.-wide pieces of plywood, centered on two adjacent edges of the first piece. These will act as locating fences for the jig. Then drill a hole in the plywood in the same position as the knob will be from the door edges. For most hardware, a $\frac{3}{16}$-in. hole works perfectly.

# resources

**For tools and cabinet hardware, pocket-hole jigs**

- **Lee Valley® Tools**
  From U.S.: (800) 871-8158
  From Canada: (800) 267-8767
  www.leevalley.com

- **McFeely's™**
  (800) 443-7937
  www.mcfeelys.com

- **Rockler® Woodworking and Hardware**
  (800) 279-4441
  www.rockler.com

- **Woodcraft®**
  (800) 535-4486
  www.woodcraft.com

- **Woodworker's Hardware®**
  (800) 383-0130
  www.wwhardware.com

- **Woodworker's Supply®**
  (800) 645-9292
  www.woodworker.com

## Further reading

- **All New Kitchen Idea Book**
  Joanne Kellar Bouknight
  The Taunton Press, Inc.

- **Building Kitchen Cabinets**
  Udo Schmidt
  The Taunton Press, Inc.

- **Building Kitchen Cabinets Made Simple**
  Gregory Paolini
  The Taunton Press, Inc.

- **Building Traditional Kitchen Cabinets**
  Jim Tolpin
  The Taunton Press, Inc.

- **Finish Carpentry**
  Editors of *Fine Homebuilding*
  The Taunton Press, Inc.

- **Kitchens for the Rest of Us**
  Peter Lemos
  The Taunton Press, Inc.

- **Kitchen Ideas that Work**
  Beth Veillette
  The Taunton Press, Inc.

- **Renovating a Kitchen**
  Editors of *Fine Homebuilding*
- The Taunton Press, Inc.

- **Taunton's Complete Illustrated Guide to Choosing and Installing Hardware**
  Bob Settich
  The Taunton Press, Inc.

- **Taunton's Trim Complete**
  Greg Kossow
  The Taunton Press, Inc.

- **Trim Carpentry**
  Clayton DeKorne
  The Taunton Press, Inc.

## Other resources

- **The Architectural Studio**
  Kitchen design and architectural services
  385 N. Haywood St., Suite 1
  Waynesville, NC 28786
  (828) 456-7529
  www.mslassoc.com

- **Architectural Woodwork Institute**
  46179 Westlake Dr.
  Suite 120
  Potomac Falls, VA 20165
  (571) 323-3636
  www.awinet.org

- **Brunner Enterprises Inc.**
  Hanging rails, panel clips, and aluminum extrusions
  455 Center Rd.
  West Seneca, NY 14224
  (877) 299-2622
  www.brunnerent.com

- **Gregory Paolini Design, LLC**
  Custom woodworking and woodworking instruction
  Waynesville, NC
  (828) 627-3948
  www.gregorypaolini.com

- **Kitchen Cabinet Manufacturers Association (KCMA®)**
  1899 Preston White Dr.
  Reston, VA 20191-5435
  (703) 264-1690
  www.kcma.org

- **True32 Flow Manufacturing**
  Bob Buckley
  196 Jefferson Pike
  LaVergne, TN 37086
  (866) 793-6420
  www.true32.com

# index